LEADING WOMEN

Jennifer Lawrence

Academy Award-Winning Actress

MADELYN BEAUREGARDE

New York

Published in 2017 by Cavendish Square Publishing, LLC
243 5th Avenue, Suite 136, New York, NY 10016

Copyright © 2017 by Cavendish Square Publishing, LLC

First Edition

No part of this publication may be reproduced, stored in a retrieval system, or transmitted in any form or by any means—electronic, mechanical, photocopying, recording, or otherwise—without the prior permission of the copyright owner. Request for permission should be addressed to Permissions, Cavendish Square Publishing, 243 5th Avenue, Suite 136, New York, NY 10016. Tel (877) 980-4450; fax (877) 980-4454.

Website: cavendishsq.com

This publication represents the opinions and views of the author based on his or her personal experience, knowledge, and research. The information in this book serves as a general guide only. The author and publisher have used their best efforts in preparing this book and disclaim liability rising directly or indirectly from the use and application of this book.

CPSIA Compliance Information: #CS16CSQ

All websites were available and accurate when this book was sent to press.

Library of Congress Cataloging-in-Publication Data

Names: Beauregarde, Madelyn, author.
Title: Jennifer Lawrence : Academy Award-winning actress / Madelyn Beauregarde.
Description: New York : Cavendish Square Publishing, 2016. | Series: Leading women | "This is Jennifer Lawrence -- That girls got talent! -- Here comes success -- They call her J-Law -- Layin' down the J-Law -- All of this was just the beginning -- Timeline -- Glossary -- Further information." |
Includes bibliographical references and index.
Identifiers: LCCN 2016005310 (print) | LCCN 2016006768 (ebook)
ISBN 9781502619853 (library bound) | ISBN 9781502619860 (ebook)
Subjects: LCSH: Lawrence, Jennifer, 1990---Juvenile literature. | Actors--United States--Biography--Juvenile literature.
Classification: LCC PN2287.L28948 B43 2016 (print) | LCC PN2287.L28948 (ebook)
DDC 791.4302/8092--dc23
LC record available at http://lccn.loc.gov/2016005310

Editorial Director: David McNamara
Editor: Elizabeth Schmermund
Copy Editor: Rebecca Rohan
Art Director: Jeffrey Talbot
Designer: Stephanie Flecha
Production Assistant: Karol Szymczuk
Photo Research: J8 Media

The photographs in this book are used by permission and through the courtesy of: Rex Features via AP Images, cover; Jennifer_Lawrence_at_the_83rd_Academy_Awards.jpg: Mingle Media TV (http://www.flickr.com/people/47170787@N05) derivative work: Tabercil (talk)/File: Jennifer Lawrence at the 83rd Academy Awards crop.jpg - Wikimedia Commons, 1; Christopher Polk/Getty Images, 4; Seth Poppel/Yearbook Library, 8; Splash News/Newscom, 10; Kevork Djansezian/Getty Images, 17, 30; VERY FUNNY PRODUCTIONS/Album/Newscom, 18; UNIMEDIA EUROPE/WILD BUNCH/Newscom, 23; ANONYMOUS CONTENT/WINTER'S BONE PRODUCTIONS/Album/Newscom, 27; © Photos 12/Alamy Stock Photo, 34; Murray Close/Getty Images, 37; © AF archive/Alamy Stock Photo, 40; Juan Sharma/Goodrich, PacificCoastNews/Newscom, 43; Jesse Grant/Getty Images for Lionsgate, 45; Beck Starr/WireImage/Getty Images, 46; © The Weinstein Company/Entertainment Pictures/ZUMAPRESS.com, 50; COLOR FORCE/Album/Newscom, 56; Neilson Barnard/Getty Images, 60; PacificCoastNews/Newscom, 62; John Lamparski/WireImage/Getty Images, 66; PETER FOLEY/EPA/Newscom, 67; © Atlaspix/Alamy Stock Photo, 70; COLOR FORCE/Album/Newscom, 74; HBE/HSS/WENN/Newscom, 79; Paul Drinkwater/NBC Universal via Getty Images, 80.

Printed in the United States of America

CONTENTS

5   **ONE:** *This Is Jennifer Lawrence*

19   **TWO:** *That Girl's Got Talent!*

31   **THREE:** *Here Comes Success*

47   **FOUR:** *They Call Her J-Law*

57   **FIVE:** *Layin' Down the J-Law*

71   **SIX:** *All of This Was Just the Beginning*

88   Timeline

90   Source Notes

97   Glossary

99   Further Information

101   Bibliography

110   Index

112   About the Author

CHAPTER ONE

This Is Jennifer Lawrence

It is the year 2013. The location: the Dolby Theatre in Hollywood, California. It is the night of the 85th Academy Awards, also known as the Oscars. Jean Dujardin, the only Frenchman to win an Oscar for Best Actor, is about to present the award for Best Actress in a Leading Role. He introduces the nominees thus: "If I were an actress, I would be passionate, sensitive, courageous, sexy, complex, free, strong, funny, intense, and graceful. If I were an actress, I would be an even better actor." He then announces the nominees: Jessica

Lawrence accepts the Oscar for her role in *Silver Linings Playbook*.

Chastain for *Zero Dark Thirty*, Emmanuelle Riva for *Armour*, Quvenzhané Wallis for *Beasts of the Southern Wild*, Naomi Watts for *The Impossible*, and Jennifer Lawrence for *Silver Linings Playbook*.

As he calls out the names, the camera cuts to each individual nominee. Each eyes the camera with a look of confident anticipation. Even ten-year-old Wallis pumps her arms up and down as he calls her name, feeding off the audience's cheers, and telling those watching to bring it on. They all seem to feel they've got this. All except one.

When the camera cuts to Jennifer Lawrence, she is wide-eyed, as if she were afraid to be seen, and appears caught off guard. She doesn't seem to fit in with this crowd or, at least, she doesn't seem to feel like she does. The woman sitting next her, her mother Karen, seems to be the confident one, almost as if she should be the nominee.

The applause dies off. A moment of silence takes its place. Dujardin opens the envelope and says, "And the Oscar goes to … Jennifer Lawrence."

She's stunned. Her hand immediately rises to cover her mouth. Presumably, Lawrence is equally floored and embarrassed by the reality that she just won the most prestigious award an actress could win in Hollywood. She might even be thinking, *This is some kind of mistake.* Actors are notorious for hamming up a performance at award shows, but there's something genuine about her reaction, and it is validated by what happens next.

This Is Jennifer Lawrence

Lawrence approaches the stage. An orchestral rendition of Stevie Wonder's *My Cherie Amour* plays—the original is featured in the film. She heads up the staircase, and then the unimaginable happens. Lawrence trips over her dress. Dujardin walks toward her and puts an arm out to help. A security guard rushes over as well and extends his arm. But Lawrence gets up by herself. All is good. No big deal. It's just a momentary **impasse**.

All the same, she takes Dujardin's hand out of courtesy, and they make their way back to the microphone together. There is a standing ovation from the crowd. They applaud not because of the incident, but for the lady standing before them. She has just won her first Academy Award, an amazing feat for a twenty-three year old. She composes herself and says, "Thank you. You guys are just standing up 'cause you feel bad that I fell."

This is Jennifer Lawrence.

From Kentucky to Tinseltown!

Jennifer Shrader Lawrence was born on August 15, 1990, to parents Gary and Karen (née Koch) Lawrence. Her father runs a contracting (construction) business. Her mother operates a summer camp on a horse farm they own outside the city. She is the youngest of three children and has two older brothers, Ben and Blaine.

Jennifer Lawrence

Lawrence was born to be in front of the camera.

This Is Jennifer Lawrence

According to an exposé on the actress from *Rolling Stone* magazine, author John Eells writes:

> *Jennifer was the first girl born on her dad's side in fifty years, and her parents raised her just like they had her two older brothers. "I didn't want her to be a diva," Karen Lawrence says. "I didn't mind if she was girlie, as long as she was tough." Jennifer was so tough that in preschool she wasn't allowed to play with the other girls because she was too rough. "She didn't mean to hurt them," her mom says. "They were just making cookies, and she wanted to play ball."*

Lawrence described her childhood on *The Late Show with David Letterman* in 2011 as "lovely" and "picturesque," but it certainly was not free of bumps and bruises. One of her first loves was horses, and she was an avid rider as a child. During the interview, David Letterman asked her if she'd ever been thrown from a horse before. Lawrence jokingly responded that she had been thrown many times because her parents hadn't wanted to pay the extra money for trained horses.

The audience laughed. There was an air of **facetiousness** in what she said, but it was clear she had a great degree of freedom as a child and spent her time running around. She also had a lot of energy.

Jennifer Lawrence

At an early age, Lawrence's brothers nicknamed her "Nitro." In 2013, talk-show host Conan O'Brien asked her where this nickname came from when she appeared on his show, *Conan*. She responded that she was called "Nitroglycerin" because she was a very hyper child, which medicine for hyperactivity didn't help.

In spite of all this horsing around, Lawrence's parents instilled a strong work ethic in their children. In 2014, while appearing on the morning chat show *Live with Kelly and Michael*, Lawrence elaborated on working at her parents' summer camp, Camp Hi-Ho, as an assistant nurse at the age of twelve, to host Kelly Ripa. She told

Lawrence's idyllic childhood home in Kentucky.

Ripa that she had always enjoyed nursing and that she had promised herself that if acting didn't work out as a career, she would go to nursing school.

However, things did work out for Jennifer Lawrence—and much sooner than she could ever have expected. But what inspired her to act? And how did she end up with an Academy Award at the age of twenty-three?

In an interview with Willa Paskin for *Glamour* magazine in 2012, Lawrence said that she never felt at home in school. There was something greater calling her, but she couldn't quite put her finger on what it was. She explained:

> I wasn't the best student. I got As and Bs, but I remember being in the classroom and looking around and being like, "Oh, all of you get this," and just feeling stupid. And then I read a script, and I just fell in love. I didn't feel stupid anymore. I just found something I was good at.

Later, Lawrence stated that she always knew that she was smart, even if she wasn't necessarily interested in academics. Once she found acting, however, she understood how she could use her intelligence—and her restlessness—to play believable characters.

Lawrence began acting at the age of nine in church plays. The very first one was based on a story from the book of Jonah. But it was when she was fourteen, and she got her hands on that first movie script, that her life really changed. The question then became whether or not her parents would allow her to follow her dream. To really pursue acting, she would have to travel to either New York City or Los Angeles, which was no small feat for a working class family of five from Louisville, Kentucky. But Lawrence was persuasive, and her mother agreed to take her to New York City for spring break that year. Lawrence hoped that she could look into talent agencies while she was there and maybe find someone who was interested in taking her on. During their trip, Lawrence and her mother stopped to watch dancers perform in Union Square. While they were watching, a man came up to Lawrence and took her photo. The man told Lawrence that he was a modeling scout, and he thought she would make a great model.

Lawrence elaborated on this meeting in an interview with journalist Diane Sawyer, saying that, at first, she and her mother were concerned about giving the man her number. However, they trusted him and soon he called Lawrence to say that modeling agencies were interested in meeting with her. Lawrence responded that she would only sign a modeling contract if she was also allowed to act—she already had her mind set at this early age.

Before the acting bug hit, Lawrence had many interests, including playing sports and cheerleading. But once she saw an opening to become an actress, nothing else mattered. She would do everything in her power to achieve her dreams.

Brothers ... a Girl's Best Friend?

Lawrence is very close with her brothers, but anyone who has siblings knows that love comes in many different forms. There was always a good amount of horsing around (both literally and figuratively) in the Lawrence household. She told David Letterman in 2013 that, when she was younger, her brothers would pin her feet behind her head and spread peanut butter all over her face. They would then lock her in the basement and sic the family's three dachshunds on her. The dogs loved peanut butter. She described this experience as "awful."

In spite of instances like this, they also had their sister's back. While her parents were unsure of letting their daughter pursue acting at first, they agreed to let her spend the next summer in New York City with her brother, Blaine. Lawrence was determined to make the most of her time: she found an agent and was able to book small parts in commercials and a couple of modeling jobs. But, before the summer was over, Lawrence's dad came to New York to take her home. He wanted her to be a normal teenager at home with her family and told her she couldn't stay in New York any longer. Reluctantly, Lawrence was ready to head back home to Kentucky when she received a call from her agent: she had gotten a part on a TV **pilot**. Now,

Lawrence was in a tough situation. She wanted to take the part, but she couldn't go against her father's wishes. This was a crucial "make or break" moment for Lawrence's career that her parents did not understand. However, her brothers did. Lawrence went on to explain what happened in *Glamour*:

> *I was a tomboy. I was the only girl, so nobody taught me how to put on a bra or wear lipstick, but my brothers [were] my biggest supporters. When I decided I wanted to act, they called my parents and were like, "You guys have been to every baseball game with us. You [have] traveled around the country going to sports games with us. This is her sport, and you have to do the same for her as you did for us." It was so great of them.*

Putting things in perspective allowed her parents to understand Lawrence's desire to act. However, sending your daughter to audition in New York or Los Angeles is more complicated than sitting in the bleachers at your sons' baseball games. The Lawrence family would need to make big changes.

Lawrence committed to finishing high school early—an entire *two years* early, in fact. And she did so with a nearly-perfect grade point average. In her spare time, she flew to Los Angeles and landed small parts in television series like *Monk*, *Cold Case*, and *Medium*.

To make it in this world, you have to start small but dream big. And that's what Jennifer Lawrence did. She explained to Conan O'Brien in a 2013 appearance on his show how small her first role on the television show *Monk* was:

> *It was really exciting, but it's also tied to the most humiliating thing in my entire life. When I was younger, we went to church every Sunday when we first moved to LA 'cause my parents were like, "Meet some friends!" They just had no idea what I would do with that opportunity. For the Monk episode, there [were these two characters], Emily J. and Emily C. I thought I was going to be playing Emily C., so this one girl [who's] in the church goes, "I'm going to be playing Emily J. in Monk!" and I was like, "Oh, my God, I'm going to be playing Emily C.! This is great!" And everyone [else] is like, "We can't wait to watch it!" [Only to] find out, I am not playing that part—I am playing the mascot. So everybody watched it after I told them that I was like going to have this great, huge part, and I was just the mascot, and I've never been back to church since.*

In Lawrence's very first appearance on screen, the audience didn't even get to see her face. She was dressed head-to-toe in a cat costume, the mascot of a high school sports team that Monk, the show's protagonist, was infiltrating. She went on to say, "They really thought I

Jennifer Lawrence

How Did You Learn to Act So Well?

Lawrence was asked this question by David Letterman on his show in 2013 after receiving her second Oscar nomination for *Silver Linings Playbook*. She responded:

> I was a big liar when I was a child … a pathological liar … I always lied about everything. I think it was, like, partly I just wanted to **one-up** somebody. Somebody would be like, "Oh God, my legs hurt." And I'd be like, "*Your* legs hurt? I'm getting mine amputated next week." And that's actually how my mother found out. She came to school and somebody was like, "God, that's such a shame about Jennifer's legs!"

Lawrence has never received any formal acting training. She is purely instinctual in her craft. Her parents maintain that the most training she received was in front of the TV as a child. "When she was a little girl, she used to just be glued to the TV," her father Gary told reporters in Louisville, Kentucky, "and I thought she was just enjoying herself, but I think she was actually studying and doing research and thinking, *I could do that.*"

"She didn't watch television like a typical child," her mother added. "She would get up on her knees and study it." Her parents were worried that this lack of formal training might stifle their daughter's career prospects, but the evidence (two Oscar nominations and two lead roles in major **franchises**) suggests otherwise.

This Is Jennifer Lawrence

The Lawrence clan (*left to right*): Ben, Jennifer, Blaine, Gary, Karen, and Ben's wife

was even lying about being the mascot." Conan assured her that being a mascot was the perfect role for her. He was right—you could see Lawrence's energy come through in her performance, and it would lead to many greater things.

CHAPTER TWO

That Girl's Got Talent!

Sometime in 2006, Jennifer Lawrence auditioned for a role that would be her big break on television. The role was that of Lauren Pearson on the debut sitcom from comedian Bill Engvall, **eponymously** titled *The Bill Engvall Show*. Lauren played the eldest child of Engvall's character. The show was about a family counselor whose family probably needed counseling themselves. It ran for thirty episodes over three seasons and received resoundingly negative reviews. Ginia Bellafante had this to say about the show in her review for the *New York Times*:

The cast of *The Bill Engvall Show*

Jennifer Lawrence

> *This brand of comedy is in the business of making fun of yuppie lifestyles and affectations, not embodying them. What is Mr. Engvall doing as a shrink in the first place? It is as if Larry David in* Curb Your Enthusiasm *started conceiving plotlines around Quaker State motor oil.*

Regardless of what the critics thought, this show propelled Lawrence to a place in the spotlight, a place she had never been before. Engvall, in particular, saw the potential in his costar. He knew that she was an up-and-coming starlet. Engvall was quoted in *The Hollywood Reporter* in 2009 as saying:

> *Of my favorite scenes that I did on that show, one of them was with Jennifer. I go back and watch it every once in a while. We had a scene where she was mad at me, and I had to go in and apologize to her. We had that nice dad-daughter moment. I remember [thinking], "This girl's good." She's got it; she's got what it takes. I think she'll be holding that statuette before she's done.*

Before the show came to an end in 2009, Lawrence started getting offers for motion pictures. The first one was *Garden Party*, a coming-of-age drama about a group of sexually-charged teenagers in Los Angeles who deal with big challenges while chasing their dreams. The film came out in 2008 and was directed by John Freeland. It starred Vanessa Shaw and Willa Holland. Lawrence had a small role as Tiff, which only garnered her a few minutes of screen time but showed that she was able to hold her own among an ensemble cast.

The Burning Plain

Lawrence's hard work was starting to pay off, insofar as she was now a blip on the radar of the film and television industry. Her next feature film role was in Guillermo Arriaga's *The Burning Plain*. It was another small role, but this time she starred alongside Charlize Theron and Kim Basinger. To perform alongside such Oscar-winning heavyweights was a huge leap forward for Lawrence's career and also an omen of things to come. The film is about a troubled teenager, played by Lawrence, who accidentally murders her mother and her mother's boyfriend, then flees to Mexico to rebuild her life. However, she finds her past troubles hard to leave behind.

Like Engvall, Arriaga knew a talented actor when he saw one. In an interview, Lawrence relayed how Arriaga had gotten in touch with her immediately after watching her audition tapes and told her she was perfect for the role. Lawrence was thrilled to be cast alongside one of her heroes, Charlize Theron. She stated that it was amazing to work alongside the older actress.

The film also presented Lawrence with another first: It was the first time she was ever nervous to act. In one scene, her character, Mariana, is shaken when she finds her mother (played by Basinger) having an affair with a man named Nick (played by Joaquim de Alemida) in their trailer. Lawrence found it difficult to prepare for such an emotionally-charged scene. In an interview, she stated:

> *I was freaking out ... before that scene. In everything that I've ever done, you can base it off yourself a little bit. I know what I look like when I cry, when I'm angry, when I'm laughing, and I can do that. So what do you do when something like that happens? I couldn't even really imagine what I could do ... and then they set up a C-stand with an "x" on it and called action. I just started shaking and crying, then it turned out to be the right choice.*

Expectations are high when you act, and part of being a screen actor is being able to perform while imagining what it is your character is actually experiencing. Making it more difficult, the shots where Lawrence's character sees her mother with Nick were not filmed with all of the actors together, so Lawrence had to pretend they were there. She pulled it off with **aplomb**, though, and everyone on the crew was pleased.

That Girl's Got Talent!

Lawrence with JD Pardo in *The Burning Plain*

Her performance was so well received, in fact, that she won the Marcello Mastroianni Award at the Venice Film Festival, which recognizes emerging actors. Jennifer Lawrence was now an award-winning actress at the age of eighteen.

The Poker House

Lawrence finally got to play a leading role in her next film, *The Poker House*, in 2009. This movie was the **directorial debut** of actress Lori Petty (the star of *Tank Girl*) and starred Selma Blair and Chloë Grace Moretz alongside Lawrence. The film tells the story of a teenage girl named Agnes (played by Lawrence) who has to raise her two younger siblings in their mother's brothel. Critics loved the film, praising the cast for depicting such a difficult story while still conveying a sense of hope.

The film was well received, as was Lawrence's performance, and it garnered her a second award: Best Performance from the Los Angeles Film Festival. A trend was starting, and Jennifer Lawrence was heading up.

At eighteen years old, Lawrence was starting to gain perspective on herself as an actor. She was also learning the value of taking on "heavy" roles, such as those in *The Burning Plain* and *The Poker House*. In an interview, she looked back on choosing to play Agnes in *The Poker House*:

> *I was young. I hadn't done anything else ... so everything that I read I wanted to do. But now that I'm older and actually have a point of view, I can see what an amazing, brilliant script it [was] ... it has teeth, and it's real, and it's ugly. When I was young, I thought it'd be fun. [When] I got it ... I just started acting. Now, I can really look back on it and appreciate it.*

This perspective allowed her to take on more mature roles, an aspect that one director in particular would use to a great degree later in her career. The days of playing the insecure daughter on a television sitcom were over. After her next role, there would be no turning back. Jennifer Lawrence was on the cusp of becoming not just an award-winning actress but also a celebrity.

Winter's Bone

Before her daughter began receiving attention for her roles, Karen Lawrence read the book *Winter's Bone* by Daniel Woodrell. She **mused** to her daughter that, should it ever be made into a film, she would be perfect for the role of the main character, Ree Dolly. The story takes place in the rural Ozarks of Missouri and is about Ree trying to locate her father to avert her family's eviction from their home. Behind the mountainous terrain lies a seedy underbelly of meth labs, secrets, and lies that Ree must pass through on her journey.

Sometime later, Lawrence received a screenplay entitled none other than *Winter's Bone*. She recognized the name, recalling her mother's enthusiasm for the book. Lawrence read it, and, as she explained in an interview with David Poland, "I fell in love with it. Actually, I became obsessed with it."

This obsession led Lawrence to pursue the film's director, Debra Granik, rather aggressively. She auditioned for the role twice for casting directors in Los Angeles but flew on a red-eye flight to New York City to find Granik and convince her in person that she was the perfect choice for the role. Lawrence told Anne Thompson in a video interview: "I would have done anything and everything to get it. I flew ... to New York to chase her and scare her. We had a very, very long audition process, and then we talked for a very long time."

Jennifer Lawrence

Her persistence paid off. It didn't take much for Granik to realize that Lawrence was the right choice for Ree Dolly. However, it did take a while to get the film financed, and it was eventually produced with a small budget of

The poster, or "one-sheet," for *Winter's Bone*

less than five million dollars. In spite of these limitations, they filmed entirely on location in the Ozarks, which contributed to the authenticity of the subject matter.

Lawrence's previous exposure to the source material also proved helpful. She told Bonnie Laufer in a video interview for *Tribute* magazine, "It was helpful to have the book. It's not very often that you get to have the inner dialogue of the character you're playing."

Also adding to the authenticity was working with locals in the Ozarks. Lawrence got to know several locals, one of whom was Ashlee Thompson, the actress who played Ree's younger sister in the film. Many of the film's scenes were filmed on the Thompson family property, so the two became quite close. In the book, Ree has two younger brothers, but those characters were changed to one brother and one sister for the film. The role of the younger brother, Sonny, was played by Isaiah Stone, another local. Lawrence explained that Granik's decision was an easy one: these terrific actors were already in the Ozarks, so they didn't need to look any further.

Lawrence also said that the locals were incredibly helpful. Granik was very meticulous about asking them questions to ensure authenticity. On working with Thompson and Stone, Lawrence said, "It was all improv because they're not actors. We wanted to make sure that they wouldn't be acting and reciting. They did it beautifully. It almost became a make-believe game that they … started to believe."

The film premiered January 21, 2010, at the Sundance Film Festival in Park City, Utah, and took the festival's award for best screenplay. It opened to widespread critical acclaim and was released in select theaters across the United States on June 11. In spite of this limited release, the word spread that it was a great film. In particular, critics and viewers alike praised Lawrence for her performance. The *Wall Street Journal* reported on June 27 that the film had done well where it had been shown, earning $84,797 in just 4 theaters during its first weekend. The *Journal* elaborated:

> [T]he movie opened to solid numbers in Overland Park, Kansas ($15,796) and St. Louis, Missouri ($12,868), where the review in the area's largest newspaper, the St. Louis Post-Dispatch, *called* Winter's Bone *"the best movie of the year." In Missouri, cities like Branson and Springfield, where independent films appear infrequently and often late in their runs, the film is holding its own in commercial theaters alongside star-studded, big-budget entries.*

Winter's Bone was a huge breakthrough for both Lawrence and Granik. The following year, it went on to garner four Academy Award nominations: Best Picture, Best Adapted Screenplay, Best Actor in a Supporting Role, and Best Actress in a Leading Role.

Jennifer Lawrence's Secret to Success

Nowadays, Jennifer Lawrence gets to be pretty picky about the scripts she chooses, but it's not always easy. This is due, in part, to the sheer volume of them floating around Hollywood. Lawrence learned early in her career that simply choosing the right one was the most important thing for her career—and it is incredibly difficult to do.

When *Tribute* magazine's Bonnie Laufer asked Lawrence if she picked such dark roles as Mariana in *The Burning Plain* or Ree in *Winter's Bone* because of any inner turmoil, she said that she chose these scripts because they were well-written and depicted complex characters. According to Lawrence, it's not easy to find a good and intelligently-written role—especially for a young, blonde actress.

One thing that Lawrence looks for in a good script is a role she can sink her teeth into. She may only get two minutes of screen time, or she may get two hours. Either way, she has learned what it takes to make an impact—by picking roles that are challenging and complex.

Guess to whom the nomination for Best Actress in a Leading Role was given?

That's right: Jennifer Lawrence.

CHAPTER THREE

Here Comes Success

The date is February 27, 2011. It is the night of the 83rd Academy Awards. The location: the Kodak Theatre in Los Angeles, California. *Winter's Bone* has been nominated in four categories, and Jennifer Lawrence is making her Oscars debut on the red carpet. She wears a simple but stunning red dress, and her long, blonde hair is down and loose. This may be her first-ever appearance at this ceremony, but she is working the scene like a pro.

Lawrence speaks with TV journalist Maria Menounos as she comes through the entry arch. They discuss that five hundred members of the press are waiting for her. Lawrence confesses it is a little

On the red carpet for the 2011 Oscars

intimidating when they scream at her. She is about to take her first stroll down a red carpet, and jokes that she's never seen such a large one before.

Her next stop is with the hosts of *Entertainment Tonight*, who comment on how fabulous she looks and how her curvaceous physique is not often seen in Hollywood. Even with the pressure to be very thin, Jennifer Lawrence has kept a realistic attitude about her body, which is a valuable asset in Hollywood. She responds to their comments by saying, "That feels great because I just ate a Philly cheesesteak, and I was kind of worried about it. People are built the way that they're built ... I think I'll be fine."

Lawrence also brings her family with her to the ceremony, something that will become a tradition. Her mother, Karen, even accompanies her daughter to speak with Ben Mulroney of *etalk*, a Canadian entertainment news show. To fill a bit of airtime, the interviewer asks the elder Lawrence what she had been reading lately, to which she replies, proudly, "I just finished reading *The Hunger Games*."

Jennifer is flabbergasted. "Oh, my God! She said it!" she cries out, and then shoos her mother away.

No matter how old you are, your parents will always be there to support and embarrass you unconditionally. They will also leak top-secret information about you to the press. Karen Lawrence had just hinted that her daughter might be involved in The Hunger Games franchise—something that would not be confirmed officially for a few more weeks.

James Franco and Anne Hathaway are the hosts for the ceremony. One of Lawrence's idols, Jeff Bridges, presents the award for the category in which she is nominated: Best Performance by an Actress in a Leading Role.

Lawrence is nominated against Annette Bening for *The Kids Are Alright*, Nicole Kidman for *Rabbit Hole*, Natalie Portman for *Black Swan*, and Michelle Williams for *Blue Valentine*. As Bridges introduces the nominees, he addresses them directly with some very kind words. He says this about Lawrence, "Jennifer, the depth you bring to the screen is well beyond your years, and I speak for everyone watching tonight when I say I look forward to watching your long career unfold."

A few moments later, he recites those famous words: "And the Oscar goes to ..." Unfortunately, it isn't followed by the name "Jennifer Lawrence." Instead, it goes to Natalie Portman. All the same, Lawrence's career has rocketed into the stratosphere, and Bridges' words confirm to everyone watching that many great things are in store for this young actress.

Jennifer Lawrence has arrived.

Two More Indies

Even though Lawrence had stepped into the mainstream arena of the Oscars, *Winter's Bone* was still an **indie film**.

Jennifer Lawrence

It was unusual for such a film to receive such critical acclaim and four Oscar nominations, and it held its own against other Best Picture contenders such as *Toy Story 3*, *Inception*, and *Black Swan*, even though it did not win in that category. And while Lawrence was about to make the jump into mainstream Hollywood "popcorn crunchers," she still loved the intimate feel of the indie world. In 2011, she appeared in two more of these films: *Like Crazy* and *The Beaver*.

Lawrence with Anton Yelchin in *The Beaver*

Like Crazy centers around a British college student who falls in love with an American man; their relationship is torn apart when she's banned from the United States for overstaying her visa. Lawrence plays the role of Samantha, the woman that the male lead falls for after his British girlfriend is sent back—and a transatlantic love triangle ensues.

The Beaver was directed by Oscar-winning actress Jodie Foster and tells the story of a troubled family man named Walter, played by Mel Gibson, who adopts a beaver hand puppet as his only means of communication. Through this puppet, his family learns a lot more than they bargained for, but it also helps them cope with all of their issues. Lawrence played Norah, the love interest of Walter's son. Lawrence told media website *Clevver TV* that this was the most normal character she has ever played, but that the character was also unexpectedly deep. She went on to say that, "[The film is] quite original, and it's touching, and it's about family, but it's not the perfect side of family, and not the perfect side of romance."

Lawrence found value in doing lower-budget and creative films like these. Because they are not financed by major studios, indie filmmakers have greater control over content and can carry out their personal artistic visions. The artistry that Lawrence valued in these films would influence her as she entered the next big phase of her career—Hollywood blockbusters.

Two Big Franchises

On March 17, 2011, eighteen days after Karen Lawrence told the world of her latest read, MTV confirmed that Lawrence was set to star as Katniss Everdeen in *The Hunger Games*, the first movie based on the popular trilogy of books by Suzanne Collins.

This wasn't the only franchise in which Lawrence would get to play a role. She had already filmed her part as Mystique, the shape-shifting mutant in *X-Men: First*

Class, which would come out that June. This would be the first of three times she would play the character, followed by *X-Men: Days of Future Past* in 2014 and *X-Men: Apocalypse* in 2016.

Lawrence explained in an interview with *Access Hollywood* that it was a big change for her to begin acting in big Hollywood movies after appearing in so many indies. But she was also excited for this new phase of her career.

X-Men: First Class was a prequel. It also served as a **soft reboot** to re-energize the X-Men franchise, which bowed out of the public eye in 2006 with the poorly received *X-Men: The Last Stand*, or *X3*. *First Class* was actually the second prequel to appear in the series. It was preceded by *X-Men Origins: Wolverine,* and both were born from a plan to make more "origin" films. It was originally developed to be *X-Men Origins: Magneto*, named for the series' primary **antagonist**, but the original plan was scrapped in favor of bringing back the X-Men team.

The film focuses on the origin of the famous X-Men characters, and follows Charles Xavier, the team's founder, who has been hit with the challenge of assembling a team of mutants to thwart the plans of his arch-nemesis Magneto to start a third World War.

Lawrence had big shoes to fill playing a younger version of Mystique, who was originally played in her adult form by Rebecca Romijn and is fondly remembered by critics and fans alike for her role. Lawrence was

Here Comes Success

Lawrence as Mystique in an X-Men film

confident she could pull it off. She told *Tribute* magazine in 2011 that the role was intriguing to her because it focused on the events that shaped Mystique's character later on.

She elaborated on this point on *Access Hollywood*, explaining that the older Mystique is more confident than the younger version: "[T]his is before when she's still an insecure young girl, kind of growing into herself, and sees it as more of a curse than a blessing. Then she kind of grows up and finds her own opinions." The character of Mystique serves as a fitting metaphor of Lawrence herself, a young woman who has honed her talents by pursuing her dreams, who has had to make a place for herself in the movie industry, always feeling a bit like an outsider. Soon, she would be expressing herself in a whole new way in Hollywood.

The most grueling part of the role for Lawrence was the makeup. Mystique, as she is portrayed in the movies, is covered head-to-toe in blue body paint and scales, representing her genetic mutation. The process took eight hours if Lawrence needed full body makeup, which shifted down to four hours for face and neck only if she got to wear clothes. Lawrence described any "head and neck" day as "a great day."

"It's kind of like a thinking man's action movie," she went on to say. "It looks cool and it's beautiful, but it's also got a great story and great character relation[ships]."

The film opened on June 3, 2011, and garnered favorable reviews, which helped it rake in $353.6 million at the box office. Lawrence was becoming a cinematic **alchemist**, turning any film in which she starred into solid gold.

But *X-Men: First Class* was just one film. The Hunger Games would be a four-film commitment with each installment shot virtually back-to-back between 2011 and 2014. Upon hearing the news that Lawrence had been cast, the books' author Suzanne Collins told MTV that, "Jennifer's just an incredible actress. So powerful, vulnerable, beautiful, unforgiving and brave. I never thought we'd find somebody this perfect for the role. And I can't wait for everyone to see her play it."

Here Comes Success

However, not everyone was pleased with this decision. Fans debated fiercely on the Internet over who should play Katniss. When Lawrence appeared as a frontrunner, many people said she was too old at twenty-one because Katniss ages from sixteen to eighteen in the books. *Entertainment Weekly's* Keith Staskiewicz addressed the matter in this way:

> *Lawrence would hardly be the first person in their twenties to play a teen: Half the high-school students on* Friday Night Lights *looked about a decade older than the other half, and the average age of* The Breakfast Club *was around 21. Heck, Gabrielle Carteris was practically in menopause when she finally stopped playing Andrea Zuckerman on* Beverly Hills, 90210. *And the Hunger Games protagonist probably* should *look a bit older than her years because, as we all know, oppressive dystopias tend to be pretty harsh on the skin.*

Filming commenced in May 2011 in North Carolina. Gary Ross, writer and director of the movies *Pleasantville* and *Seabiscuit*, helmed the first installment. He adapted the book to film along with Collins and screenwriter Billy Ray.

The Hunger Games takes place in the dystopian society of Panem, built out of the ashes of a ruined America. Each year, the districts that make up the country must select two "tributes," one boy and one girl, to compete in the Hunger Games, a televised spectacle where children compete to the death. Katniss Everdeen volunteers from District 12 to keep her younger sister from going. After falling for her fellow tribute, Peeta, she must use her cunning instincts to win the games and keep them both alive.

Even though The Hunger Games books were virtually brand new, having been released between 2008 and 2010, they had, by 2011, acquired a large and dedicated fan base. Director Gary Ross understood that the expectations were high, and he had a plan to serve the fans. He felt the best way to approach the movie was by making it as

Katniss volunteers herself as tribute in the first installment of *The Hunger Games*

subjective and personal as possible. The best way to do this was to make audiences experience the events of the film as intensely as possible through the eyes of Katniss Everdeen. The only way to accomplish this was to cast a top-notch actress to sling the bow and arrow.

And what was it exactly that attracted Lawrence to the role? Lawrence stated: "It was this futuristic *Joan of Arc* and … when you look what's on reality television … and [the idea of] history repeating itself, it's actually incredibly relevant. I thought it was a very important story to be told."

Once again, Lawrence's discerning taste in scripts led her to pick the perfect role.

Gettin' Tough!

Lawrence trained extensively for the shoot. She hit the gym with a personal trainer and learned to shoot a bow and arrow—a key strength of Katniss Everdeen's—from Olympian archer Khatuna Lorig.

During her training, Lawrence developed a whole new respect for the sport, having to shoot hundreds of arrows a day. She mentioned in interviews that archery is a very difficult sport, but, once you get the hang of it, it is really fun. Lawrence also said the worst part of shooting arrows was getting whipped inside the arm by the bow if she wasn't paying attention. But Lawrence is used to punishment, having survived multiple scuffs with horses on her parents' farm and growing up in the suburban wilds of Louisville. Ultimately, it was nothing she couldn't handle.

Her personal trainer, Dr. Joe Horrigan, told *Teen Vogue* in 2014: "Jennifer was an utmost professional. She was never late. She never missed a workout. She never complained. She did everything that was asked of her, and she usually did so with a smile."

Ross was also pleased with Lawrence, but he knew she would be great from the get-go. He worked hand-in-hand with Collins to choose the actress who would play Katniss, and they both agreed that Lawrence was the right choice. He told *Entertainment Weekly* that choosing her over all the other candidates was "the easiest casting decision I ever made." Elaborating on this, he said:

> *First, I saw* Winter's Bone, *and I just thought she was phenomenally talented and just kind of riveting and amazing and had so much power. And then we had a meeting, and I found her to be just a completely compelling, intelligent person. But then she came in and read for me, and it just knocked me out. I don't want to go into too many details, but we did a scene from the movie, and it was so amazingly powerful that it was sort of stunning.*

The film was set to premiere on March 23, 2012—exactly one year and five days after Karen Lawrence "announced" her daughter would play Katniss. Leading

Here Comes Success

Lawrence rehearses an action scene in *The Hunger Games*.

up to the premiere, Lawrence, co-star Josh Hutcherson, and several other cast members embarked on a promotional "mall tour," stopping at shopping malls in eight major cities: Atlanta, Chicago, Dallas, Los Angeles, Miami, Minneapolis, Phoenix, and Seattle.

Lawrence was front and center at the majority of these appearances, followed by Hutcherson. She survived her first Oscars, no problem, but this was something else. This was her first exposure to **fandom**. These weren't just interviewers on the red carpet, these were fans screaming for Katniss Everdeen. Lawrence, who is generally very gracious and laid back in her interviews, was noticeably agitated by the fanfare. At the Mall of

Jennifer Lawrence

Jennifer Lawrence, Scream Queen!

Jennifer Lawrence has starred in serious dramas; she's starred in action films; she's even starred as a blue-skinned, shape-shifting mutant in a series of superhero films, but did you know that she is also a certified scream queen? Lawrence starred in an oft-overlooked picture called *House at the End of the Street*, a horror film about a woman (played by Elizabeth Shue) and her teenage daughter (played by Lawrence) who move into a new house, only to find out the house down the way has a terrible secret: it was once the site of a grisly double murder. Things begin to unravel when she befriends a boy in the neighborhood who happens to be the sole survivor of that fateful night.

"It was something completely different than I had ever done," Lawrence said about the film. "I liked that there were so many twists with the characters, and you didn't know who you could trust. You spend the whole movie wondering."

This film provided Lawrence with a new challenge: Acting alone. Her character spent a lot of the time being pursued by the killer, so throughout the movie, she was by herself. "There's a lot more thinking on your feet," she said. "If you have a big scene with another actor, [you] can always … rehearse it, but how in the world are you going to rehearse running upstairs screaming and crawling on the floor?"

And how did Lawrence handle the pressure? With confidence, just as she had done in *The Burning Plain*. She learned to rely on her instinct because every performance would be different. Lawrence ran through all of the scenes in her head, first, with the understanding that it all could change the moment the director calls action.

Here Comes Success

Liam Hemsworth, Lawrence, and Josh Hutcherson autograph posters for a fan.

America in Minneapolis, the event's host asked the cast members how they were enjoying their day.

Lawrence's response was that the event was very loud. Her answer was characteristically blunt, but unusually **perturbed**. The other cast members chimed in and offered up much more enthusiastic responses to keep the crowd pumped.

There were certainly adjustment pains leading up to the film's Los Angeles premiere. But, soon, Lawrence got used to her newfound fame. She told interviewers at the premiere that she was enjoying her fans' excitement.

Just in the nick of time, Jennifer Lawrence was her old self again.

CHAPTER FOUR

They Call Her J-Law

In 2004, fourteen-year-old Jennifer Lawrence was just beginning to toy with the idea of becoming an actress—someday—if only her parents would let her. Meanwhile, a forty-six-year-old filmmaker named David O. Russell was about to release his fourth feature film, entitled *I Heart Huckabees*. The film was written and directed by Russell and starred a powerhouse cast for the time: Dustin Hoffman, Lily Tomlin, Jude Law, Mark Wahlberg, Naomi Watts, and Jason Schwartzman.

The film came out at a time when like-minded (and similarly budgeted) indie films were the style du jour, with such hits as *Eternal Sunshine of the Spotless Mind* and *Closer* (both released in 2004). In contrast to these

David O. Russell signs a special one-sheet for *Silver Linings Playbook*.

two films, however, *I Heart Huckabees* bombed at the box office. The film earned $20.1 million worldwide, a figure just above the film's $20 million budget—essentially breaking even.

Russell's reputation was damaged by the film's poor performance, but the death knell came in 2007 when a video went **viral** showing Tomlin and him engaging in an explosive argument on set. Although the video came out three years after the film, it underscored the terse goings-on behind the scenes.

Russell would not direct again for six more years. Hollywood is not much for second chances, but occasionally miracles happen. In 2010, he made a film called *The Fighter*, which—while hardly a comeback—would put him back in the director's chair and allow him to shop around other projects at a pace worthy of an A-list Hollywood director.

But that wasn't his miracle. That came just after *The Fighter*. The miracle was embodied in a particular actress who was breaking through that very same year. That miracle's name, of course, was Jennifer Lawrence.

Lawrence had her agent reach out to Russell regarding his next project. Lawrence wanted in, but everyone involved thought she was too young for the part—the opposite issue she faced when accused of being "too old" to play Katniss Everdeen. That did not stop her from setting up a meeting, however. She elaborated on their initial encounter to YouTube channel *DP/30: The Oral History of Hollywood*:

> *I've been a huge David O. Russell fan since I started learning about film, and my agents knew this, and there was this movie, and they weren't considering me because [I was] way too young. And I just ... went on Skype and met with David and [then] went to New York and ... forced him to hire me.*

Russell explained that he did not feel that Lawrence was a contender at first. He was already talking to three other actresses who were more established in the industry, one of which was Angelina Jolie. He felt that Lawrence was too young for the role, considering its complexity.

In spite of his concern, Lawrence showed him via that Skype call just how serious she was about working with him and playing the part. She auditioned from her parents' house and dressed up like the character, complete with hair and makeup. She even went as far as killing a real spider that had startled her — in character. Russell told *On Demand News* that he was "knocked out." He saw that "she was completely committed to the character."

Russell was sold. The role she auditioned for was Tiffany. The film was *Silver Linings Playbook*.

Silver Linings Playbook

Silver Linings Playbook is the story of a former teacher named Pat (played by Bradley Cooper) who, after doing time in a mental institution, tries to reconnect with his parents and ex-wife—but things begin to fall apart

Jennifer Lawrence

when he meets a mysterious woman named Tiffany. This culminates in two bets being wagered: One involving a football game between Pat and his father, and the other involving a ballroom dancing contest between Pat and Tiffany, which she forces him into.

Lawrence and co-star Bradley Cooper struck up quite the friendship during filming. Rumors even surfaced that they were dating, but this was resolutely denied by all parties involved. Regardless, the chemistry was there, and Russell was pleased by it. On a "making of" featurette for the film, he described Lawrence as "amazing . . . an extraordinary, gifted, scary actress," and said that she and Cooper had "a fantastic, easygoing chemistry together."

Russell found that she was able to play someone older than herself with ease, even coming off The Hunger Games. He described her as having "an emotional intuitiveness and intensity that just comes across."

Lawrence and Bradley Cooper about to dance in *Silver Linings Playbook*

Russell was entering a new phase in his career, and so was Lawrence. He was (and still is) grateful to have her on board. The feeling was mutual. Lawrence elaborated on this in an interview:

> *I am the luckiest person in the entire world to do what I do. I've been really lucky with everybody that I've worked with. I haven't worked with any nightmares. Everybody I've that worked with so far has been really wonderful and down to earth.*

She went on to say that working with Russell was "like a dream come true." She was such a huge fan of his that she didn't want to build it up too much in her head. She prepared herself to be let down, but found out while working with him that he "was the nicest, warmest, sweetest person in the entire world" and that he had a good energy.

And, when asked about the "age issue," Lawrence said: "It's just going to be one those things. People are just going to have to accept it."

Donna Gigliotti, producer of *Silver Linings Playbook*, also complimented Lawrence's performance. She said: "It's chemical with this girl. That's all I can say. At twenty-one years old, she is absolutely the most staggering talent I've seen come along in Hollywood in a very long time."

Silver Linings Playbook opened on November 18, 2012. It had a budget of $21 million, slightly more than *I Heart Huckabees*, but unlike its predecessor it brought in $236.4 million at the box office. It was a huge hit and received overwhelmingly positive reviews. Critics and viewers alike were particularly fond of Lawrence and Cooper's performances—and their onscreen chemistry.

On January 10, 2013, the Academy of Motion Picture Arts and Sciences, the governing body of the Oscars, announced its nominees for its 85th annual award ceremony. The film was nominated in eight categories: Best Picture, Best Director, Best Actor (Bradley Cooper), Best Actress (Jennifer Lawrence), Best Supporting Actor (Robert De Niro), Best Supporting Actress (Jacki Weaver), Best Adapted Screenplay, and Best Film Editing.

Out of those eight categories, only Jennifer Lawrence took home the statue.

American Hustle

Russell, Cooper, and Lawrence would collaborate again in 2013 on the director's next project: *American Hustle*. Experiencing a career renaissance, Russell considered Cooper and Lawrence, along with others in his "family" of actors, to be good luck charms.

Roger Ebert elaborated on this in his review of the film, saying, "[Russell] has always has shown a fondness for characters who are on the brink of imploding or exploding. But he's so skilled with these actors, he not only finds a side to them we haven't seen in his previous films, he finds a side we haven't seen, period."

American Hustle is about a couple of con artists (played by Christian Bale and Amy Adams) who infiltrate the seedy underbelly of New Jersey powerbrokers and the Mafia in the 1970s. Lawrence plays Bale's unhinged wife, whom he is afraid to leave for fear of losing contact with his adopted son. Cooper plays an FBI agent who coaxes the con artists into getting more arrests in exchange for their freedom.

Initially, Lawrence did not want to do the movie. Her schedule was already jam-packed. At first, she wanted some time off, which she explained in an interview with ABC News: "I wanted to go on vacation. I didn't want to want to do the movie. But I had so many ideas that I would get so excited about, and it was one of the most creative, stimulating times of my life."

Russell was fortunate to have Lawrence in his armada of actors. He saw this film as the next installment of a series, including *The Fighter* and *Silver Linings Playbook*, all of which were thematically linked. He explained to *Entertainment Weekly* at a ceremony held in his honor by the American Film Institute on November 8, 2013, that he wanted to create "a similar world of people, and a family, and a community, and a home, who speak a certain way, and who are emotional, and very intense," which he said he finds "fascinating". He went on to say that *American Hustle* was "the biggest world in a way ... an extension of these salt-of-the-earth, soulful people trying to survive." According to him, this is what all these films are about.

Jennifer Lawrence

Codename: J-Law, or The Many Nicknames of Jennifer Lawrence

Her family might call her Nitro, but the world knows her as J-Law. But where did the nickname J-Law come from? You might think an overzealous media that loves to shorten celebrity names invented it for their own nefarious ends. Lindsey Lohan is LiLo. Jennifer Lopez is J.Lo—not a far cry from J-Law. The media even goes so far as to make **portmanteaus** of celebrity couples: Ben Affleck and Jennifer Lopez became Bennifer. He later married Jennifer Garner, and they were also Bennifer, or Bennifer 2.0. Brad Pitt and Angelina Jolie became Brangelina. This list goes on.

Believe it or not, the name J-Law predates her fame. Lawrence's teacher, Mr. Noah, first bestowed it upon her in the seventh grade, and she does not mind it at all.

On a recent trip to China, Lawrence learned during a **Q&A** session that they have an entirely different nickname for her over there: Big Elderly Cousin. She told this to Conan O'Brien during an interview in November 2015, stating that she was flattered by this nickname. While this might sound like a term of endearment, it is, in fact, supposed to be humorous. CNN uncovered the meaning behind it: in the run-up to the Oscars in 2011, many Chinese fans claimed they had heard the results of the show before it ever aired—and that Lawrence had won—because they all had a "big elderly cousin" in the Academy who gave them the scoop. Well, their *biao jie* (Chinese for "cousin") lied to them! She wouldn't win an Oscar until 2012. But the name stuck and is now counted among Lawrence's many nicknames.

But the real question is: Do you spell it J.Law, J-Law, or JLaw? It seems to be just a matter of preference.

The film was released December 13, 2013, to positive critical acclaim. Ebert praised the film in his review as well, saying, "*American Hustle* is a character study at its core—an exploration of dissatisfaction and drive, and the lengths to which we're willing to go for that elusive thing known as a better life."

Manohla Dargis of the *New York Times* elaborated on this, noting that, "Russell ... has reinvigorated [the] **screwball comedy**, partly by insisting that men and women talk to one another. To that end, that chatter ... is fast, dirty, intemperate, hilarious, and largely in service to the art of the con."

This time, the film was nominated for *ten* Academy Awards: Best Picture, Best Director, Best Actor (Christian Bale), Best Actress (Amy Adams), Best Supporting Actor (Bradley Cooper), Best Supporting Actress (Jennifer Lawrence), Best Original Screenplay, Best Film Editing, and additionally Best Costume Design and Best Production Design.

However, on the night of the 86th Academy Awards on March 2, 2014, the film did not take home a single statue. While still an important stepping stone in Lawrence's career—an Oscar win is, by no means, a measure of a film's worth—the Academy's decision not to acknowledge the film could be seen as an indirect omen of things to come, for Lawrence's career was about to make an unexpected left turn.

CHAPTER FIVE

Layin' Down the J-Law

Jennifer Lawrence was now a respected actress, franchise icon, and Oscar winner. This **trifecta** put her in an usual position for a twenty-two year old. How would she use her newfound fame? Was there something more to this success? Did she possess a deeper purpose underneath her public **persona**? These questions may not have crossed her mind in 2012. But something changed in Hollywood just three years later that would cause these questions to surface.

In addition to *American Hustle* in 2013, Sony also produced a film called *The Interview* about an assassination attempt on North Korean dictator Kim

Katniss shows off her wedding dress to Caesar Flickerman (Stanley Tucci).

Jung-Un. The film starred Seth Rogan and James Franco and was a **satirical** comedy. However, a group of **hackers** failed to find the humor in it and used the film as a reason to hack the company's computer servers. While the hackers claimed to be from North Korea, this was never proven. Some people speculated that it was an inside job. Regardless, the **cyber attack** led to the release of one of the largest "data dumps" of confidential information in history. Among the documents released were e-mail correspondences, personal information of employees (such as home addresses and Social Security numbers), and actors' **salaries**.

Sony temporarily shelved *The Interview*, amidst the chaos, which curbed its success, and fired their chairwoman, Amy Pascal. This scandal also led back to Lawrence, who saw the hacked information on actors' salaries—including her own. She noticed something alarming: male actors were making more money than their female contemporaries. More specifically, Jeremy Renner, one of the lead actors in *American Hustle*, had been paid more than either Lawrence or their co-star Amy Adams.

Lawrence had the opportunity to voice her opinions via Lena Dunham's online newsletter, *Lenny*, in an essay entitled, "Why Do I Make Less Than My Male Co-Stars?" She expressed anger at herself for not being a better negotiator. It wasn't that she *couldn't* have been paid more. It was that she stopped short of asking for a higher salary due to a fear of being judged. She blamed this on the cultural stigmas of being a woman seen and not heard. "I didn't get mad at Sony. I got mad at myself," she wrote. "I didn't want to keep fighting over millions of dollars that, frankly, due to two franchises, I don't need." She continued, saying:

> *But if I'm honest with myself, I would be lying if I didn't say there was an element of wanting to be liked that influenced my decision to close the deal without a real fight. I didn't want to seem "difficult" or "spoiled." At the time, that seemed like a fine idea, until I saw the payroll on the Internet and realized every man I was working with definitely didn't worry about being "difficult" or "spoiled."*
>
> *If anything, I'm sure they were commended for being fierce and tactical, while I was busy worrying about coming across as a brat and not getting my fair share. Again, this might have nothing to do with [being female], but I wasn't completely wrong when another leaked Sony email revealed a producer referring to a fellow lead actress in a negotiation as a "spoiled brat." For some reason, I just can't picture someone saying that about a man.*

The e-mail Lawrence referred to was between Pascal and producer Scott Rudin, and they were talking about actress Angelina Jolie. Pascal claimed that Jolie wasn't bothered by the quip, saying that, "Everybody understood because we all live in this weird thing called Hollywood.

Jennifer Lawrence

Former Sony Pictures chairwoman Amy Pascal

If we all actually were nice, it wouldn't work." It was also revealed that Pascal was the only woman at Sony's corporate office making over one million dollars a year.

Lawrence's choice to speak out about income inequality would propel her fame to yet another level.

Controlling Your Stock

The very same day that Lawrence's essay went live, news surfaced that she had bowed out of starring in *The Rosie Project*, based on the novel by Graeme Simsion. *The Rosie Project* tells the story of a genetics professor who cannot seem to have meaningful relationships with a member of the opposite sex. With the help of a friend, he develops a questionnaire to assess the suitability of female partners.

This brings an intriguing woman named Rosie into the picture, who doesn't meet any of the criteria—and throws his plan completely off course. Lawrence was up for playing the eponymous female lead. The reason for her departure was because Sony was unwilling to pay her the same amount she had been offered on another project at the studio, *Passengers*, co-starring Chris Pratt (star of *Guardians of the Galaxy* and *Jurassic World*). That amount was twenty million dollars.

Lawrence maintained that she was willing to take a pay cut to work with Richard Linklater, who would be directing the film, but the negotiations dragged on, and they were unable to reach amicable terms. Interestingly enough, Sony's negotiations were handled by Thomas Rothman, Pascal's replacement. Linklater's contract was handled quickly, another point of frustration for Lawrence, and she was said to have lost interest in the project. After Lawrence left, so did Linklater, and the project is currently shelved.

Lawrence spoke further about this with Diane Sawyer on ABC's *Nightline*, citing statistics that women are paid, on average, twenty-one percent less than men. She explained that asking for equal pay is even more difficult for women than for men because women often are deemed money-hungry or too aggressive. Men, she continued, are often not judged by the same standards and are praised for being assertive enough to ask for the money they deserve.

Lawrence went on to state the fundamental reason why she spoke out on pay inequality in the interview:

Jennifer Lawrence

Lawrence reminisces with Diane Sawyer at New York City's Union Square.

"Controlling your stock, if you will, and being in control of that. I love acting—that's the only part of my job that I love—but all of it's a business." For Lawrence, speaking about equal pay is not just important in the film industry, but is important no matter what career path you choose. She makes sure to tell her fans that it is important to take charge of their professional lives whether they are male or female and to make sure that they are being treated fairly.

The Backlash

Although her message was inspirational, Lawrence received some backlash for speaking her mind. In particular, Lawrence was criticized for speaking out about pay inequality as a woman who had the privilege of making multiple millions on each of her film projects. For some critics, Lawrence was disconnected from the daily struggles of most women who were paid only a fraction of what Lawrence made and struggled to support themselves and their families. They spoke out against Lawrence, arguing that it was not appropriate for her to complain about her salary when she made so much.

In particular, writer Kristin Ross was vocal about her criticism of Jennifer Lawrence and her call for pay equality between the sexes. In an article entitled "Thanks, Hollywood, But I Don't Care What You Have to Say About Pay Inequality," she wrote:

> [Lawrence's] reaction is that of a privileged 1-percenter whose salary is in the millions of dollars range, and whose perk-filled pampered life is light years beyond most in this country. I also enjoy how she stomps her feet in disgust, but then verbally shrugs it off, because she's already doing so well.

But Lawrence stood firm. In an interview with Jordan Riefe, Lawrence addressed these criticisms by saying, "If a woman speaks up and is assertive and has a voice, she's going to be called a brat." She expressed that gender inequity is not limited to Hollywood, but that such pay inequality exists throughout the United States, and that she hoped to lend more attention to the issue in speaking about it. Although the Equal Pay Act, which states that businesses cannot pay employees differently based on their sex, was passed in 1963, Lawrence's struggle shows that women are still offered lower salaries than men and are often viewed in a more negative light if they ask for more.

The Rosie Project aside, Lawrence was able to negotiate a higher pay rate for subsequent projects, including *Passengers* and the later installments in the

Jennifer Lawrence

Hunger Games film series. She's now one of the top earners in Hollywood, making between ten and twenty million dollars per film.

The lasting effect of Lawrence's essay on pay inequity remains to be seen. Only time will tell if her publicized battle for fair pay will encourage more women to speak out. However, it has certainly gotten the conversation started. Even David O. Russell came out publicly and supported her. In an interview with writer Ashley Lee, he said:

> *I always support all my actors and all their opinions, and I want them all to get what they need. I don't really talk about the minutia of what goes on in my movies, but I believe the spirit of what Jennifer is saying is truthful ... It's hard to make a movie come together with a lot of big stars.* American Hustle *had a lot of big stars in it. We all contributed to help make it happen.*

Russell went on to compare Lawrence to the character she plays in *Joy*, their third and most recent collaboration: "[Her] character in *Joy* is about the same thing: Maturity, learning what it is to have your own space and express your own voice and to have power. And that's what she's learning."

Lawrence's *American Hustle* costar Bradley Cooper was also supportive of her, stating that he would like to help female costars in the future negotiate their pay rates. He went onto say, "if you think that you only deserve a certain amount, and that's not correct, it's about changing that mindset and sticking up for yourself. That's a great thing."

However, one of Lawrence's costars took a different approach to her publicized criticism of Hollywood's salaries: Jeremy Renner, the costar who **purportedly** made more on the film than any other actor. In an article for *Business Insider*, writer Jason Guerasio quoted the star as saying, "I don't know contracts and money and all that sort of stuff. I'm a performer and I know human behavior. When it comes to that sort of stuff, I let other people deal with that. I do what I'm good at, that's what I focus on." This response seemed to deny that there was a larger problem as to why women were offered lower salaries than their male counterparts. Renner later clarified his comments in this interview and stated that he supported female actresses who fought for pay equality.

In 2015, *Forbes* magazine listed Lawrence as the highest-paid actress in Hollywood, and listed her earnings as $52 million for the year. *Business Insider* reported that Lawrence beat actress Scarlett Johansson, who earned $35.5 million during the same period. The article also noted that Lawrence has increased her earnings from 2014 to 2015 by $18 million. Following Lawrence and Johansson were Melissa McCarthy in third place with $23 million, Jennifer Aniston in fourth place with $16.5 million, and Angelina Jolie in seventh

Jennifer Lawrence

Lawrence with the men of *American Hustle* (*left to right*): Christian Bale, Bradley Cooper, and Jeremy Renner

with $15 million. Altogether, the top ten highest-paid actresses on the list earned a combined $206 million in 2015. The top ten men on the list, which included Robert Downey Jr. at number one with $80 million and Bradley Cooper at number four with $41.5 million, earned a combined $431 million—more than double their female counterparts. On average, the top ten men made $43.1 million, while actresses only made $20.6 million.

One source of this problem is the distribution of something called "points"—percentage points of the profits a film makes that go to actors on the back end. *Forbes* reported that Lawrence and Amy Adams made seven percent in points, while Cooper, Bale, and Renner all made nine. *Forbes* noted that "while Lawrence may have had a smaller role than her male counterparts, back-end compensation is typically awarded based on star power and gravitas, which Lawrence possesses on par with Bale and Renner."

Other actresses have voiced their frustrations as well. At the 2015 Oscars, Patricia Arquette spoke out about the matter during her acceptance speech for Best Supporting Actress (for the film *Boyhood*). Charlize Theron, also a subject of the Sony email hack, was able to negotiate a higher rate for her role as villainous Ravenna in the sequel to *Snow White and the Huntsman*. Sources say it was to the tune of ten million dollars.

While Lawrence has gone on to become the top-grossing actress in Hollywood, she has gained a lot of support in regard to pay inequity from fellow actresses. Lena Dunham, who gained attention through her TV series, *Girls*, is no stranger to controversy herself and

Lena Dunham, Lawrence's friend and guru

Jennifer Lawrence

J-Law Gives Back to the Kids

Income inequality is not the only cause Jennifer Lawrence has taken up. Propelled by the success of Winter's Bone, Lawrence was able to give back to the community of Louisville, Kentucky, where she grew up. She became the spokesperson for Bellewood Home for Children when asked to be guest of honor at its 2011 Youth Film Festival. Bellewood, which now operates under the name Uspiritus, is an orphanage that provides social services for abused, vulnerable, and homeless youth.

"It means a lot for [Lawrence] to support Bellewood," a spokesperson for Bellewood said in a video produced by the organization. "For her to do a Q&A with them, and to show them that she's just like them, and that there's a commonality amongst all of us."

"I think it's inspiring to the kids to have someone like Jennifer come out," said Robert Bertrand, another representative of Bellewood, in an interview with WHAS 11 in Louisville, "and her film tells the story of what these kids have been through."

"Nothing that's worth it is going to be handed to you," Lawrence told the kids during the Q&A. She hoped that speaking with the children of Bellewood would inspire them. She also has a personal connection to the institution: her grandfather volunteered his time to play Santa Claus there, her aunt taught horseback riding there, and her family's Camp Hi-Ho is accessible to the residents.

All proceeds from the Louisville premiere of Winter's Bone were donated to Bellewood as well.

has spoken out about women's rights and feminism extensively in the media. She's also the mastermind of *Lenny*, the e-mail newsletter in which Lawrence's essay first appeared, and a friend of Lawrence's. Dunham spoke to *Entertainment Weekly* online about Lawrence:

> I think what Jen did that's so great in the letter is that she talked about ... making less [and] about the desire to be likable and how that interferes with our ability as women to advocate for ourselves ... she took that approach to examine the industry [and] examine the societal factor, the fact that we raise our girls [in a way] that causes them to ask for less than they are worth.

Lawrence is certainly changing the game. In taking on pay inequality in Hollywood, Lawrence has become a role model for the young girls who look up to her. She is an example of a powerful actress who has struggled with being treated differently because of her gender, has spoken out candidly about those struggles, and then fought for greater equality in her own life, and in the lives of others. Time will tell what her greatest role will be, although it is quite possibly the work she has done off-screen in the fight for pay equality in Hollywood.

CHAPTER SIX

All of This Was Just the Beginning

Jennifer Lawrence has shown no signs of slowing down. She has been at the top of her game since her 2013 Oscar win. By the end of 2015, she had wrapped up the final installment of The Hunger Games movies, *The Hunger Games: Mockingjay Part 2*, which was released on November 16, 2015. Also in time for the holidays—and the ensuing award season—was *Joy*, her third collaboration with David O. Russell.

However, the film business is tricky, and not even Lawrence is immune to the ebb and flow of public opinion and box office receipts.

Lawrence shed a tear with Robert De Niro in *Joy*.

Jennifer Lawrence

The first installment of The Hunger Games series made a huge splash with $694.4 million in box office returns. The first sequel, *The Hunger Games: Catching Fire*, did even better, raking in $865 million. But then things began to change. The third installment, *The Hunger Games: Mockingjay Part 1*, only brought in $755.4 million, and the fourth, *Mockingjay Part 2*, only $652.9 million. Analysts suspected the public might be tiring on the franchise, especially because the third book in the trilogy was split into two films. *Mockingjay Part 2* was also up against the blockbuster *Star Wars: The Force Awakens*. When that film opened on December 18, *Mockingjay Part 2* became an afterthought.

That being said, The Hunger Games films were by no means a disaster. The franchise ended up putting Jennifer Lawrence in the *Guinness Book of World Records* after all, and its total worldwide gross is more than the gross domestic product of many countries. Brent Lang put things in perspective in an article for *Variety*:

> *Despite falling short of outsized expectations, Hunger Games remains a Tiffany franchise. It dispelled the old myths that audiences wouldn't accept action films with female leads. It proved that pictures without superheroes can inspire fan bases that are as fervent and devoted as those of* The Avengers *or* The Dark Knight. *And it cemented Jennifer Lawrence's status as the most bankable actress of her generation at a time when star power is at its* **nadir.**

All of This Was Just the Beginning

There has been a charge of female-driven franchises in the past decade, and The Hunger Games series is undoubtedly the movement's lynchpin. First came Kristen Stewart in the Twilight saga, which put the idea on the map that a strong female protagonist could carry a series of genre films. However, it was Lawrence in The Hunger Games that really gave the movement its legs—and its muscle. It inspired imitators such the Divergent series and MTV's The Shannara Chronicles. While all of these series began as books at different points in time, it was their adaptations to visual media that really delivered the concept to the masses. Both the books and the movies have set a positive precedent, which arguably culminated in 2015's *Mad Max: Fury Road,* a film that took an established franchise with a male lead and put him in the back seat. This film focused on Furiosa, a female character played by Charlize Theron, who starred in *The Burning Plain* with Lawrence several years before.

In her interview with *Nightline's* Diane Sawyer, Lawrence explained what she hopes people will take away from the series: "I ... just hope that there's no longer a separation ... of, 'Oh, it's a female-driven movie,' or, 'Oh my God, it's a blockbuster, but it was led by a woman,' or, 'Wow, that was a really tough call for a woman.'" This is especially important in Hollywood, where women are often pigeonholed into traditional female roles.

After the four Hunger Games films, Lawrence is ready to move on, despite how much she enjoyed making

Jennifer Lawrence

Katniss at the climax of *The Hunger Games*

them. Lawrence prioritized these films for four years over everything else—including her personal life. She told Sawyer, "Being twenty-four was this whole year of, 'Who am I without these movies? Who am I without this man?'"

The end of making *The Hunger Games* movies coincided with the end of another period in Lawrence's life—her longtime relationship with fellow actor Nicholas Hoult. This breakup would force Lawrence to reevaluate her own priorities in life just as her career was taking off.

Nicholas Hoult

Jennifer Lawrence is very career-oriented. As a woman in her midtwenties, she considers work to be more important than play. She became romantically involved with *X-Men: First Class* co-star Nicholas Hoult during filming, and the couple were together on and off for about five years. The split was amicable, and the two remain friends, but it was the hectic pace of their lives that caused the breakup. Both are successful actors and, as such, their careers take up most of their time.

"When we're busy, we agree to mutually ignore each other," she told *Marie Claire* magazine in 2014. "Not completely, but neither of us gets mad when the other doesn't text back or call. Life's super busy. Obviously you know what they're doing, and you trust them."

Regardless, the pressure of maintaining a relationship on top of that was too much. It finally took its toll. However, Lawrence explained to Diane Sawyer that she feels good about the direction her career and personal life have taken. She stated, "I don't know if I ever will get married, and I'm okay with that. I don't feel like I need anything to complete me. I love meeting people, people coming into my life and bringing something."

A Joy-ful Christmas Day

Hot on the heels of *Mockingjay Part 2* was *Joy*, which came out on Christmas Day 2015. The film tells the story of Joy Mangano, creator of the Miracle Mop, and her journey from being a down-on-her-luck single mother to a selfmade millionaire through her inventiveness, business sense, and drive. Against all odds, her invention became one of the first real successes of the QVC/Home Shopping Network boom of the 1990s.

"What I loved about Joy is that I found her whole journey very inspiring," Lawrence stated in an interview. "She was told 'no' a million times, and she had this burning desire. We take her from when she believes in herself and no one else does to when other people start to believe in her."

One could make the argument that Lawrence saw herself in the character of Joy, as a woman from meager beginnings with a burning desire to succeed, who achieves her dreams through a hard work ethic. For Russell, the film was about so much more.

"[The film] is about the soul of someone," he said, "and what is in the soul of that person, and what moves them to stay stuck or trapped, or what moves them to break out and create something new, not only for themselves, but for everybody around them." He went on to say that he liked how joy, the emotion, shifts throughout the course of the film as the character Joy transforms into a fiercer person to achieve her dreams.

Lawrence went on to explain that the most fascinating part of the movie, for her, was that it featured a powerful female lead and did not revolve around a romance.

What makes *Joy* such a wonderful film is that it is about one woman's perseverance against the odds and how she learns to overcome them, simply by being herself. She learns to trust her instincts and to find her own self-confidence by listening to herself and not to others. QVC executive Neil Walker, played by Cooper, tells her that his company only uses celebrities to sell their products and tells Joy she can't do it herself—but he doesn't succeed in selling one single mop. Only when Joy insists that she appear on TV do things start to change. Walker also tries to make her wear outfits that fit the QVC **aesthetic**, but she chooses instead to wear what she always wears when working around the house: a simple button-down shirt and slacks. This simple outfit proves to be a successful way to market her mops, too.

As inspired as the cast was to make the movie, rumor holds that all was not well on set. Reports surfaced in February 2015 of an intense screaming match between Russell and Lawrence in the same vein as the director's row with Lily Tomlin in 2004. According to one report, Russell screamed at her in a way that was "ear-piercing and laced with profanities." However, an executive at Fox 2000, the production company behind the film, said this was just "method acting" and part of the process in which a director communicates with his actors.

The rumors snowballed in the media, prompting Lawrence to make a rare "personal appearance" on her Facebook page to put the matter to rest. She posted the following on February 27, 2015:

Jennifer Lawrence

> *I know I don't go on here a lot because I can barely work email, but there's been a terrible rumor going around the last 24 hours, so I wanted to clear it up.*
>
> *David O. Russell is one of my closest friends, and we have an amazing collaborative working relationship. I adore this man, and he does not deserve this tabloid malarkey. This movie is going great and I'm having a blast making it!*

Lawrence is never afraid to speak her mind, especially in response to media reports that often blow things out of proportion. In speaking directly to the people who matter the most to her—her fans—Lawrence shows how much she values them, all while incorporating her trademark wit into an otherwise touchy subject.

But Is She His Muse?

Whatever tension may or may not have existed on set, Russell and Lawrence have a long-standing and intimate professional relationship. Russell has even alluded to the fact that Lawrence is his muse. Russell claims that he doesn't just write parts for Lawrence, but that he is inspired in his writing and directing by her.

"If you really have a soul connection with someone, you tend to reproduce it," Russell has said, referring to his consistent collaboration with Lawrence. "Sometimes you have a kinship with someone … we share a sense of

All of This Was Just the Beginning

Lawrence and David O. Russell strut their stuff at the 2016 Golden Globe Awards.

humor. We share a sense of what we cry about. We share a sense about what we love. We really like each other and like to laugh together and have fun."

The film garnered two Golden Globe nominations heading into awards season: Best Motion Picture—Musical or Comedy, and Best Actress—Musical or Comedy for Lawrence. It only received one Academy

79

Jennifer Lawrence

Award nomination: Best Actress in a Leading Role for Lawrence. She won just the Golden Globe. Regardless, it is safe to say that *Joy* will not be the last of their collaborations.

Amy Schumer, Jennifer's Muse?

Coincidentally, Lawrence was nominated in the same category as both her best friend, Amy Schumer (star of Judd Apatow's *Trainwreck*), and Lily Tomlin (for her role as Elle in Paul Weitz's *Grandma*). There was no official comment from Tomlin, but she and Russell put their grievance to rest years ago. They both have stated publicly that they admire each other's work and wish each other

Lawrence and Amy Schumer, feuding friends?

the best. Schumer, however, came out swinging against her best friend. She told *Entertainment Weekly*: "As soon as I saw that we were both nominated, I took her right out of my phone because our friendship is obviously over. It's really every woman for herself at this point."

Schumer was joking, of course. They're still friends. They are also writing a screenplay together wherein they will play sisters. No title or any further information has been released, but Lawrence spoke enthusiastically about the project in an interview with Brooks Barnes at *The New York Times*:

> *Amy and I were creatively made for each other. We have different flavors. It's been the most fun experience of my life. We start the day off on the phone, laughing. And then we send each other pages. And we crack up. I'm flying out tomorrow to see her in Chicago. We'll write a little bit with her sister, Kim, who worked with Amy when she was writing* Trainwreck.

That trip to Chicago was not all business. On August 27, 2015, the actresses took time out of their busy schedules to see Billy Joel perform at Wrigley Field. He invited them onstage during "Uptown Girl"—and they got to dance on his piano! The song features prominently in *Trainwreck,* and the girls' appearance caused quite a stir with the fans.

The antics didn't stop there. Lawrence joked the she and Schumer were trying to figure out how to wear the same thing to the Golden Globes. People took her seriously, but she was just kidding around. In all seriousness, though, Lawrence hoped that members of the Hollywood Foreign Press would vote for Schumer—she really wanted to see her best friend take home the award. She spoke openly about this to Seth Meyers on his show, *Late Night*: "Her performance was the year. She was the year. She drew the map, she wrote it out, she put herself on it, and then she showed us the map. That's who I would vote for." Unfortunately, or fortunately, depending on who you ask, Lawrence beat out Schumer.

Lawrence and Schumer became friends rather recently, although they haven't spoken publicly about how they met. Media outlets only found out about their burgeoning friendship after they took a vacation together in the Hamptons in the summer of 2015. Schumer posted a photo of them together on a yacht with a group of friends forming a human pyramid. This created a media firestorm where stories about their relationship were churned out almost daily. What draws people to their friendship is what fans love about each of them: they are both opinionated, boisterous, and completely in control of their careers.

Days of Future Past

In 2014, Lawrence starred in a sequel to *X-Men: First Class* entitled *X-Men: Days of Future Past*. It was the seventh installment in the series and marked the return of Bryan Singer to the director's chair. He had previously helmed the first two films: *X-Men* (2000) and *X2: X-Men United* (2003). Singer is regarded as the most popular *X-Men* director as the first two films, in particular *X2*, are considered the best of the series.

Lawrence reprised her role as the blue-skinned and sultry Mystique, whose character contributed to a pivotal plot point in the film. The film centers around the X-Men being sent back in time in order to change history and prevent a timestream-altering occurrence from changing the present for both human- and mutant-kind.

The film was a critical and financial success. Although certainly not Hunger Games-level, it proved to be another access point for Lawrence to enter the world of "comic book nerd" culture. Both franchises have allowed her to sit in on multiple panels at San Diego Comic-Con—much to the delight of fans everywhere.

The success of these two films led to her contractual option to appear in one more installment. Three is the magic number, after all. The third film, *X-Men: Apocalypse*, is about the resurrection of the first

Jennifer Lawrence

Accolades

Jennifer Lawrence has become a box office sensation due to her three Oscar nominations, but these aren't the only awards she's been nominated for. Starting with *Winter's Bone*, she has been honored with a constant stream of accolades across the globe.

Los Angeles's Film Independent Spirit Awards and New York City's Gotham Awards were the first to recognize the rising star in 2010 for *Winter's Bone*. She did not win either award, but she did win as part of Best Ensemble Performance from the Gotham Awards.

The Hollywood Foreign Press has nominated her for its Golden Globe Awards and the Hollywood Press Academy for its Satellite Awards. Both organizations nominated her for Best Actress for *Winter's Bone* and *Silver Linings Playbook*, and Best Supporting Actress for *American Hustle*. She won the Satellite in 2012 for *Silver Linings Playbook* and the Golden Globe for *Silver Linings Playbook* and *American Hustle*.

However, nothing beats the love she has received from the MTV Movie Awards. The television channel has nominated her a whopping eighteen times for six films from 2012 to 2015. MTV offers a wide array of award categories at its show, and Lawrence has been nominated three times for Best Kiss, twice for Best Fight, and once for being the most scared in the horror film *House at the End of the Street*.

But these are hardly the most unique awards she has received. In 2015, the *Guinness Book of World Records* honored Lawrence's portrayal of Katniss Everdeen as the

All of This Was Just the Beginning

Lawrence at the world premiere of *The Hunger Games*

Highest Grossing Action Heroine of all time. This has nothing to do with how much she made personally on the films but, rather, is based on The Hunger Games' movies total gross earnings of $854 million worldwide. Not bad for a twenty-five-year-old from Kentucky!

mutant, the eponymous supervillain Apocalypse, who was worshipped as a god in ancient times. He grows disillusioned with the modern world and seeks to destroy it by recruiting his own team of mutants, the Four Horsemen.

Does Jennifer Lawrence plan to play Mystique in any further installments beyond this one? At first, it seemed that Lawrence would leave the franchise as she publicly declared that *X-Men: Apocalypse* would be her last.

Then, in June 2015, she gave slightly different response during an interview with *Entertainment Weekly*: "There is hope," she said. "I don't want to not be asked."

And what was the reason for leaving? Lawrence said that she enjoyed working with Singer and loves the movies, but it was the grueling makeup schedule, especially the exposure to all the chemicals, that made her think she wouldn't come back after all. The more she went through the process, she said, the more she wondered if it was good for her.

Now that The Hunger Games movies are complete, she has also stated publicly that she probably won't return for any additional sequels or prequels either. She told *Variety* that, "I wouldn't be involved. I think it's too soon. They've got to let the body get cold, in my opinion."

Perhaps, given enough time, she will return to both franchises. Only time will tell.

Whatever her plans, the future looks bright for Jennifer Lawrence. But her impressive career hasn't come easy. It took a lot of hard work and determination to get where she is today. In fact, it took almost ten years to achieve that Oscar win from the moment she began seriously acting. A popular expression holds that it takes fifteen years to become an overnight success, and Jennifer Lawrence made it in just over a decade.

And how has she handled this success? Lawrence told *Vanity Fair* in 2013: "Why would I ever get cocky? I'm not saving anybody's life. There are doctors who save lives, and firemen who run into burning buildings. I'm making movies." Lawrence has kept her success in perspective, which, in itself, is not an easy feat in Hollywood, where successful actors and actresses are often worshipped like gods. Lawrence has maintained her laid-back attitude to this day, stating, "I'm a big believer of accepting yourself and not really worrying about it."

Lawrence's confidence stems from one very simple practice: above all, she believes in herself. And, without the fear of failure that plagues many people, Lawrence continues to achieve greater and greater things as one of the most well-liked and respected actresses in Hollywood today.

Timeline

1999 — Lawrence begins acting in church plays.

2009 — Lawrence auditions for the role of Ree Dolly in *Winter's Bone*, is originally turned down and then convinces the casting director that she would be perfect for the role.

1990 — Jennifer Lawrence is born on August 15.

2007 — *The Bill Engvall Show*, Lawrence's first big gig

2004 — Lawrence travels to New York City for the first time, where she is discovered.

2012

The Hunger Games is released on March 23.

2015

Lawrence's essay, "Why Do I Make Less Than My Male Co-Stars?" is published in *Lenny* on October 14. *Forbes* magazine lists Lawrence as the highest-paid actress in Hollywood, earning $52 million for the year.

2010

Winter's Bone is released on June 11; this becomes Lawrence's breakthrough role.

Lawrence is nominated for her first Academy Award for her role in *Winter's Bone*. She does not win.

2011

Lawrence wins her first Academy Award for *Silver Linings Playbook*; her relationship with actor Nicholas Hoult ends.

2013

SOURCE NOTES

Chapter One

Page 7: "Jennifer Lawrence Wins Best Actress: 2013 Oscars," www.youtube.com/watch?v=WDU7zLAd2-U

Page 9: Eells, Josh, "Jennifer Lawrence: America's Kick-Ass Sweetheart," *Rolling Stone*, April 12, 2012. www.rollingstone.com/movies/news/jennifer-lawrence-americas-kick-ass-sweetheart.

Page 11: Paskin, Willa, "Interview with Jennifer Lawrence." *Glamour*, March 6, 2012. www.glamour.com/story/get-a-sneak-preview-of-glamour-1.

Page 11: "'Hunger Games' Jennifer Lawrence Talks About Katniss & Picking Boyfriends - Glamour Cover Stars," *Glamour*, March 1, 2012, www.youtube.com/watch?v=8WFv8vPuPJE.

Page 15: "Jennifer Lawrence's Big Break Was As A Mascot On 'Monk' - Conan on TBS," YouTube video, February 6, 2013, www.youtube.com/watch?v=lgb0x-oNzg5w.

Page 16: "Jennifer Lawrence Interview with David Letterman," YouTube video, January 21, 2013, www.youtube.com/watch?v=eoLfRlkOQVI.

Page 17: "(Part 1) Jennifer Lawrence's family sits down with WDRB," YouTube video, March 22, 2013, www.youtube.com/watch?v=ky2hefeMlZ4.

Chapter Two

Page 20: Bellafante, Ginia, "Dad Is in Control at Work, but He Is in Deep Chaos at Home," *New York Times*, July 17, 2007. http://www.nytimes.com/2007/07/17/arts/television/17bell.html.

Page 20: Zakarin, Jordan, "Jennifer Lawrence's Career Journey, From 'Bill Engvall' to 'Hunger Games,'" *The Hollywood Reporter*, March 22, 2012. http://www.hollywoodreporter.com/heat-vision/jennifer-lawrence-career-bill-engvall-winters-bone-hunger-games.

Page 22: Movie Geeks United! "Rare JENNIFER LAWRENCE Interview," YouTube video, April 14, 2012, www.youtube.com/watch?v=9YvUuv1yAo4.

Page 24: Sawyer, "Jennifer Lawrence on Life After 'Hunger Games,' Fighting for Fair Pay."

Page 25: Paskin, "Interview with Jennifer Lawrence."

Page 25: TributeMovies, "Jennifer Lawrence - Winter's Bone Interview," YouTube video, June 8, 2010, www.youtube.com/watch?v=Hv7Sgrt_PXo.

Page 27: DP/30: The Oral History Of Hollywood, "Winter's Bone, actor Jennifer Lawrence," YouTube video, September 3, 2011, www.youtube.com/watch?v=YdmzElDO2ic.

Page 28: Kaufman, Anthony, "Box Office Focus: 'Winter's Bone' Heats Up in the Heartland," *Wall Street Journal*, June 27, 2010. blogs.wsj.com/speakeasy/2010/06/27/box-office-focus-winters-bone-heats-up-in-the-heartland.

Chapter Three

Page 32: "Oscars Red Carpet Live," YouTube video, March 17, 2012, www.youtube.com/watch?v=Snt-WYRT_Ztk.

Page 32: Oscars. "Natalie Portman Winning Best Actress." YouTube video, www.youtube.com/watch?v=BYvUm1YJBSs.

Page 37: "Interview of Jennifer Lawrence about X-Men First Class by *Access Hollywood*," YouTube video, March 20, 2011, www.youtube.com/watch?v=Os-9mIIqlJYU

Page 38: *Ibid.*

Page 38: Wilkinson, Amy, "'Hunger Games' Casting Exclusive: Lionsgate Confirms Jennifer Lawrence As Katniss," *MTV*, March 17, 2011. www.mtv.com/news/2555422/hunger-games-jennifer-lawrence-lionsgate-confirms.

Page 39: Staskiewicz, Keith, "'Hunger Games': Is Jennifer Lawrence the Katniss of your dreams?" *Entertainment Weekly*, March 17, 2011. www.ew.com/article/2011/03/17/jennifer-lawrence-too-old-katniss-hunger-games.

Page 42: Tejeda, Valerie, "Jennifer Lawrence's Personal Trainer Gave Us Her Full 'Hunger Games' Workout Routine," *Teen Vogue*, July 1, 2014. www.teenvogue.com/story/jennifer-lawrence-hunger-games-workout-tips.

Page 42: Valby, Karen, "'Hunger Games' director Gary Ross talks about 'the easiest casting decision of my life,'" *Entertainment Weekly*, March 17, 2011.

Page 44: MyMovieTrailers, "House At The End of The Street - Jennifer Lawrence on the Story," YouTube video, September 16, 2012, www.youtube.com/watch?v=obtutUx-vt8.

Page 44: BlockbusterUK, "House at the End of the Street Movie Feature Cast Interviews," YouTube video, September 11, 2012, www.youtube.com/watch?v=zy6EQb3J3Yw.

Chapter Four

Page 49: On Demand News, "David O. Russell talks about Jennifer Lawrence's next project, her first audition & his film-making," video, March 1, 2014, www.youtube.com/watch?v=k9ZZM3bHp4o.

Page 50: Russell, David O.,. "Silver Linings Playbook - 'Making Of' Featurette (Jennifer Lawrence),." YouTube video, 12:27. July 17, 2014, . www.youtube.com/watch?v=Gb71T1khjx8.

Page 51: "David O Russell and Jennifer Lawrence: 'American Hustle,'" YouTube video, July 15, 2014, www.youtube.com/watch?v=VLgpickHHJw

Page 51: *Ibid*.

Page 55: Ebert, Roger, "American Hustle review," Rogerebert.com, 2013, www.rogerebert.com/reviews/american-hustle-2013.

Page 55: Dargis, Manohla, "Big Hair, Bad Scams, Motormouths," *New York Times*, December 12, 2013. http://www.nytimes.com/2013/12/13/movies/american-hustle-with-christian-bale-and-amy-adams.html.

Chapter Five

Page 59: Lawrence, Jennifer, "Why Do I Make Less Than My Male Co-Stars?" *Lenny*, October 14, 2015. http://www.lennyletter.com/work/a147/jennifer-lawrence-why-do-i-make-less-than-my-male-costars.

Page 62: Lewis, Hilary, "Jennifer Lawrence Talks 'Submissiveness,' How She 'Would Love to See Change' in Pay Gap," *The Hollywood Reporter*, November 12, 2015. www.hollywoodreporter.com/news/jennifer-lawrence-talks-submissiveness-how-839649.

Page 63: Ross, Kimberly, "Thanks, Hollywood, But I Don't Care What You Have to Say About Pay Inequality," *Red State*, October 17, 2015. www.redstate.com/kimberly_ross/2015/10/17/thanks-hollywood-dont-care-say-pay-inequality.

Page 63: Riefe, Jordan, "Jennifer Lawrence Explains Gender Pay Gap Remarks," *The Hollywood Reporter*, November 4, 2015. www.hollywoodreporter.com/news/jennifer-lawrence-explains-gender-pay-837200.

Page 74: Lee, Ashley, "David O. Russell on Jennifer Lawrence's Wage-Gap Gripe: It's Hard to Make Deals "With a Lot of Big Stars," *The Hollywood Reporter*, November 22, 2015.

Page 65: Guerrasio, Jason, "Jeremy Renner" *Business Insider*, October 20, 2015. www.businessinsider.com/jeremy-renner-on-gender-pay-gap.

Page 65: Berg, Madeline, "Everything You Need To Know About The Hollywood Pay Gap," *Forbes*, November 12, 2015. www.forbes.com/sites/maddieberg/2015/11/12/everything-you-need-to-know-about-the-hollywood-pay-gap.

Pages 66-67: Li, Shirley, "Lena Dunham praises Jennifer Lawrence for wage gap essay," *Entertainment Weekly*, October 28, 2015. www.ew.com/article/2015/10/28/lena-dunham-jennifer-lawrence-hollywood-wage-gap-lenny.

Page 68: Bellewood Home for Children, "Bellewood Loves You, Jennifer Lawrence," YouTube video, February 24, 2011, www.youtube.com/watch?v=WdT-sOXPJ1l.

Page 69: JenniferLawrenceVideos, "Celebrity Star Jennifer Lawrence Visits Children." YouTube video, June 29, 2010, www.youtube.com/watch?v=Vz9gFGWW-W_Y.

Chapter Six

Page 72: Lang, Brent, "Hunger Games: Mockingjay – Part 2 is a Smash Hit, So Why the Disappointment?" *Variety*, November 22, 2015. variety.com/2015/film/box-office/hunger-games-mockingjay-part-2-box-office-disappointment.

Page 73: Sawyer, "Jennifer Lawrence on Life After 'Hunger Games,' Fighting for Fair Pay."

Page 74: *Ibid*.

Page 75: Gell, Aaron, "Jennifer Lawrence Just Can't Help It," *Marie Claire*, May 7, 2014, http://www.marieclaire.com/celebrity/a6589/jlaw.

Page 75: Sawyer, "Jennifer Lawrence on Life After 'Hunger Games,' Fighting for Fair Pay."

Page 76: Film4, "Interview: Jennifer Lawrence & David O. Russell talk Joy," YouTube video, December 27, 2015, www.youtube.com/watch?v=i_y0PZ01Q34.

Page 76: Film4, "Interview: Jennifer Lawrence & David O. Russell talk Joy."

Page 78: Lawrence, Jennifer, Facebook post, February 27, 2015,www.facebook.com/JenniferLawrence/posts/10152564822511793.

Page 78: "Women In The World Conversation with David O. Russell, Jennifer Lawrence and Joy Mangano," YouTube video, December 17, 2015.

Page 81: Coggan, Devin, "Amy Schumer: Jennifer Lawrence friendship 'obviously over' after competing Globes nods." *Entertainment Weekly*, December 10, 2015. www.ew.com/article/2015/12/10/golden-globes-2016-amy-schumer-trainwreck-jennifer-lawrence.

Page 82: Barnes, Brooks, "Jennifer Lawrence and Amy Schumer Writing Screenplay Together," *New York Times*, August 26, 2015. artsbeat.blogs.nytimes.com/2015/08/26/jennifer-lawrence-amy-schumer-writing-screenplay-together/.

Page 86: Late Night with Seth Meyers, "Jennifer Lawrence on Her Friendship with Amy Schumer," YouTube video, December 16, 2015, www.youtube.com/watch?v=6S3XcyHxUgw

Page 86: Coggan, Devin, "Amy Schumer: Jennifer Lawrence friendship 'obviously over.'"

Page 87: Stack, Tim, "Jennifer Lawrence on possibility of returning to X-Men franchise: 'There is hope,'" *Entertainment Weekly*, July 17, 2015. www.ew.com/article/2015/07/15/x-men-apocalypse-star-jennifer-lawrence-leaving-franchise-hope.

GLOSSARY

aesthetic A particular vision or look implemented by an artist.

alchemist Someone who has the ability to change one thing into something else in a very impressive way.

antagonist The person working against the main character in a story, sometimes a villain.

aplomb Showing confidence, especially in a difficult situation.

cyber attack An attack waged by a group of hackers on a network or computer system.

directorial debut A director's first film.

eponymously Used to describe something that is named after its central character or creator.

facetiousness Speaking humorously at a possibly inappropriate time.

fandom A population of fans.

franchise A story that is explored in a series of films, books, or other media.

hackers Individuals who break into a computer system to gain access to data that is not their own.

impasse A predicament with no obvious outcome.

indie film A film made outside of Hollywood, usually with a small budget.

muse To speak in a thoughtful way.

nadir The lowest point in someone or something's existence.

one-up To gain an advantage over someone.

persona The personality that a person presents to others.

perturbed To be upset about something.

pilot The first episode of a new TV show, used to test if audiences will like it.

portmanteau Blending two words into one.

purportedly Said to be true by the person who experienced it.

Q&A A question and answer session.

salaries The amount of money someone makes for a duration of time.

satirical Using humor to discredit something that is considered normal.

screwball comedy A film with a particularly over the top or zany bent to its humor.

soft reboot A film that takes place in the same universe as previous films or books, but change the original story line in some way.

trifecta The best three.

FURTHER INFORMATION

Books

Higgins, Nadia. *Jennifer Lawrence: The Hunger Games' Girl on Fire.* Minneapolis, MN: Lerner Classroom, 2013.

Jennifer Lawrence: Burning Bright. Chicago, IL: Triumph Books, 2013.

Morreale, Marie. *Jennifer Lawrence.* New York, NY: Scholastic Books, 2015.

Websites

The Jennifer Lawrence Foundation
jenniferlawrencefoundation.com
This website for the Jennifer Lawrence Foundation includes promotional videos for Lawrence's films, a list of upcoming events, and links to the charities that Lawrence supports.

The Longest-Running Jennifer Lawrence Fan Site
jennifer-lawrence.com
The longest-running fan site for Jennifer Lawrence includes news, a detailed biography, videos, and a list of films the actress has acted in.

Videos

"Jennifer Lawrence Interrupted by Jack Nicholson at Oscars"
www.youtube.com/watch?v=WJmhsJ5T5L0
In this video, actor Jack Nicholson interrupts Lawrence's post-Oscars interview with reporter George Stephanopolous to congratulate her on her win.

"Jennifer Lawrence on Life After 'Hunger Games,' Fighting for Fair Pay"
www.youtube.com/watch?v=HonXlE21lwo
Diane Sawyer's interview with Jennifer Lawrence on ABC's *Nightline*.

BIBLIOGRAPHY

20th Century Fox. "JOY | Women In The World Conversation with David O. Russell, Jennifer Lawrence and Joy Mangano." *YouTube* video, 36:00. December 17, 2015.

ABC News. "Jennifer Lawrence on Life After 'Hunger Games,' Fighting for Fair Pay." *YouTube* video, 9:22. November 13, 2015. www.youtube.com/watch?v=HonXlE21lwo.

Barnes, Brooks. "Jennifer Lawrence and Amy Schumer Writing Screenplay Together." *New York Times*, August 26, 2015. artsbeat.blogs.nytimes.com/2015/08/26/jennifer-lawrence-amy-schumer-writing-screenplay-together.

Bellafante, Ginia. "Dad Is in Control at Work, but He Is in Deep Chaos at Home." *New York Times*, July 17, 2007. www.nytimes.com/2007/07/17/arts/television/17bell.html .

Bellewood Home for Children. "Bellewood Loves You, Jennifer Lawrence." *YouTube* video, 4:00. February 24, 2011. www.youtube.com/watch?v=WdTsOXPJ1l

Berg, Madeline. "Everything You Need To Know About The Hollywood Pay Gap." *Forbes*, November 12, 2015. www.forbes.com/sites/maddieberg/2015/11/12/everything-you-need-to-know.

BlockbusterUK. "House at the End of the Street Movie Feature Cast Interviews." *YouTube* video, 2:28. September 11, 2012. www.youtube.com/watch?v=zy6EQb3J3Yw

Clevver Movies. "Jennifer Lawrence 'The Beaver' Interview." *YouTube* video, 3:21. April 21, 2011. www.youtube.com/watch?v=mGYd7n8-S9A

Clevver TV. "Jennifer Lawrence - The Hunger Games Premiere Interview." *YouTube* video, 0:29. March 13, 2012. www.youtube.com/watch?v=z5XRSaPMVzY

Coggan, Devin. "Amy Schumer: Jennifer Lawrence friendship 'obviously over' after competing Globes nods." *Entertainment Weekly*, December 10, 2015. www.ew.com/article/2015/12/10/golden-globes-2016-amy-schumer-trainwreck-jennifer-lawrence.

Dargis, Manohla. "Big Hair, Bad Scams, Motormouths." *New York Times*, December 12, 2013. www.nytimes.com/2013/12/13/movies/american-hustle-with-christian-bale-and-amy-adams.html.

DaveRyanShow. "101.3 KDWB Interviews *The Hunger Games* Cast at Mall of America." *YouTube* video, 9:50. www.youtube.com/watch?v=pTypPPIjSPc.

DP/30: The Oral History of Hollywood. "Jennifer Lawrence @ TIFF 2012 - Silver Linings Playbook." *YouTube* video, 31:07. September 18, 2012. https://www.youtube.com/watch?v=Gh2TDgitYcQ.

———. "Winter's Bone, actor Jennifer Lawrence." *YouTube* video, 30:36. September 3, 2011. www.youtube.com/watch?v=YdmzElDO2ic.

Ebert, Roger. "*Silver Linings Playbook* review." Rogerbert.com, 2012. www.rogerebert.com/reviews/silver-linings-playbook-2012.

———. "*American Hustle* review." Rogerebert.com, 2013. www.rogerebert.com/reviews/american-hustle-2013.

Eells, Josh. "Jennifer Lawrence: America's Kick-Ass Sweetheart." *Rolling Stone*, April 12, 2012. www.rollingstone.com/movies/news/jennifer-lawrence-americas-kick-ass-sweetheart-20120412.

Epstein, Daniel. "David O. Russell interview." *SuicideGirls.com*, October 5, 2004. suicidegirls.com/girls/anderswolleck/blog/2679051/david-o-russell/etalk.

CTV. "The Katniss Hunger Games frontrunner: Jennifer Lawrence." YouTube video, 1:03. March 2, 2011. www.youtube.com/watch?v=hfeocDoZn6o.

Film4. "Interview: Jennifer Lawrence & David O. Russell talk Joy." *YouTube* video, 9:42. December 27, 2015. www.youtube.com/watch?v=i_y0PZ01Q34.

Glamour Magazine. "'Hunger Games' Jennifer Lawrence Talks About Katniss & Picking Boyfriends - Glamour Cover Stars." YouTube video, 2:36. March 1, 2012. www.youtube.com/watch?v=8WFv8vPuPJE.

Guerrasio, Jason. "Jennifer Lawrence named the world's highest-paid actress." *Business Insider*, August 20, 2015. www.businessinsider.com/jennifer-lawrence-is-worlds-highest-paid-actress-of-2015-2015-8.

_____. "Jeremy Renner, who starred in 'American Hustle' with Bradley Cooper and Jennifer Lawrence, says it's 'not my job' to help female co-stars negotiate higher salaries." *Business Insider*, October 20, 2015. www.businessinsider.com/jeremy-renner-on-gender-pay-gap-2015-10.

hdtv00. "Oscars Red Carpet Live." *YouTube* video, 3:22. March 17, 2012. www.youtube.com/watch?v=Snt-WYRT_Ztk.

Higgins, Nadia. *Jennifer Lawrence: The Hunger Games' Girl on Fire*. Minneapolis, MN: Lerner Classroom, 2013.

Kaufman, Amy. "The embarrassing emails that preceded Amy Pascal's resignation." *Los Angeles Times*, February 5, 2015. www.latimes.com/entertainment/envelope/cotown/la-et-ct-amy-pascal-email-rogen-hirai-20150205-story.html.

Kaufman, Anthony. "Box Office Focus: 'Winter's Bone' Heats Up in the Heartland." *Wall Street Journal*, June 27 2010. blogs.wsj.com/speakeasy/2010/06/27/box-office-focus-winters-bone-heats-up-in-the-heartland.

Lang, Brent. "*Hunger Games: Mockingjay — Part 2* is a Smash Hit, So Why the Disappointment?" *Variety*, November 22, 2015.

Lang, Brent. "Jennifer Lawrence on 'Hunger Games' Prequels: 'It's Too Soon.'" *Variety*, December 13, 2015. variety.com/2015/film/news/jennifer-lawrence-hunger-games-prequels-1201660189.

Late Night with Seth Meyers. "Jennifer Lawrence on Her Friendship with Amy Schumer." YouTube video, 3:01. December 16, 2015. www.youtube.com/watch?v=6S3XcyHxUgw.

JenniferLawrenceVideos. "Celebrity Star Jennifer Lawrence Visits Children." *YouTube* video, 2:35. June 29, 2010. www.youtube.com/watch?v=Vz9gFGWWW_Y.

——————. "Interview of Jennifer Lawrence about X-Men First Class by Access Hollywood." YouTube video, 4:00. March 20, 2011. www.youtube.com/watch?v=Os9mIIqlJYU.

——————. "Jennifer Lawrence on The Late Show with David Letterman." *YouTube* video, 6:47. May 20, 2011. www.youtube.com/watch?v=nSW00RiLMSs.

Lawrence, Jennifer. Facebook post, February 27, 2015. www.facebook.com/JenniferLawrence posts/10152564822511793.

——————. "Why Do I Make Less Than My Male Co-Stars?" *Lenny*, October 14, 2015. www.lennyletter.com/work/a147/jennifer-lawrence-why-do-i-make-less-than-my-male-costars.

Lee, Ashley. "David O. Russell on Jennifer Lawrence's Wage-Gap Gripe: It's Hard to Make Deals "With a Lot of Big Stars." *The Hollywood Reporter*, November 22, 2015.

Lewis, Hilary. "Jennifer Lawrence Talks 'Submissiveness,' How She 'Would Love to See Change' in Pay Gap." *The Hollywood Reporter*, November 12, 2015.

Li, Shirley. "Lena Dunham praises Jennifer Lawrence for wage gap essay." *Entertainment Weekly*, October 28, 2015.

Matthew, Sam. "Angelina didn't care she was called a spoilt brat in leaked emails, claims disgraced Sony executive Amy Pascal — that's just how we behave in Hollywood." *The Daily Mail*, February 12, 2015.

Mendelson, Scott. "*Hunger Games* Box Office: Why $101M Weekend For *Mockingjay 2* May Be Cause For Despair." *Forbes*, November 22, 2015.

Morreale, Marie. *Jennifer Lawrence*. New York, NY: Scholastic Books, 2015.

MovieClipsComingSoon. "*The Hunger Games* - Jennifer Lawrence Interview (2012) HD Movie." *YouTube* video, 6:35. March 12, 2012. www.youtube.com/watch?v=-82jYp0TU0XY

Movie Geeks United! "Rare JENNIFER LAWRENCE Interview." *YouTube* video, 15:50. April 14, 2012. www.youtube.com/watch?v=9YvUuv1yAo4

MyMovieTrailers. "House At The End of The Street - Jennifer Lawrence on the Story." *YouTube* video, 0:52. September 16, 2012. www.youtube.com/watch?v=obtutUx-vt8

On Demand News. "David O. Russell talks about Jennifer Lawrence's next project, her first audition & his film-making." YouTube video, 7:30. March 1, 2014. www.youtube.com/watch?v=k9ZZM3bHp4o

Oscars. "Jennifer Lawrence Wins Best Actress: 2013 Oscars." *YouTube* video, 2:36. www.youtube.com/watch?v=WDU7zLAd2-U

———. "Natalie Portman Winning Best Actress." *YouTube* video, 6:31.

Paskin, Willa. "Interview with Jennifer Lawrence." *Glamour*, March 6, 2012.

Riefe, Jordan. "Jennifer Lawrence Explains Gender Pay Gap Remarks." *The Hollywood Reporter,* November 4, 2015.

Roberts, Sheila. "Interview: Jennifer Lawrence and Director Lori Petty on *The Poker House*." *Collider*, July 17, 2009.

Ross, Kimberly. "Thanks, Hollywood, But I Don't Care What You Have to Say About Pay Inequality." *Red State*, October 17, 2015.

David O. Russell. "*Silver Linings Playbook* - 'Making Of' Featurette (Jennifer Lawrence)." *YouTube* video, 12:27. July 17, 2014. www.youtube.com/watch?v=Gb71T1khjx8

———. "David O Russell and Jennifer Lawrence:

'American Hustle.'" *YouTube* video, 2:17. July 15, 2014. www.youtube.com/watch?v=VLgpickHHJw.

Stack, Tim. "Jennifer Lawrence on possibility of returning to X-Men franchise: 'There is hope.'" *Entertainment Weekly*, July 17, 2015. http://www.ew.com/article/2015/07/15/x-men-apocalypse-star-jennifer-lawrence-leaving-franchise-hope.

Staskiewicz, Keith. "'Hunger Games': Is Jennifer Lawrence the Katniss of your dreams?" *Entertainment Weekly*, March 17, 2011. www.ew.com/article/2011/03/17/jennifer-lawrence-too-old-katniss-hunger-games.

TeamCoco. "Jennifer Lawrence's Big Break Was As A Mascot On 'Monk' - Conan on TBS." *YouTube* video, 4:54. February 6, 2013. www.youtube.com/watch?v=lgb0xoNzg5w.

_____. "Jennifer Lawrence's Weird Chinese Nickname." YouTube video, 2:16. November 20, 2015. https://www.youtube.com/watch?v=AoqhMBUNNbg.

Tejeda, Valerie. "Jennifer Lawrence's Personal Trainer Gave Us Her Full 'Hunger Games' Workout Routine." *Teen Vogue*, July 1, 2014. www.teenvogue.com/story/jennifer-lawrence-hunger-games-workout-tips.

Thompson, Anne. "Jennifer Lawrence 1." *YouTube* video, 6:40. October 27, 2010. www.youtube.com/watch?v=P-6nOH02Kd1s.

Tony Jamison. "Jennifer Lawrence Interview - Live with Kelly and Michael." YouTube video, 9:43. May 23, 2014.

www.youtube.com/watch?v=Edz_81y0vp0.

TributeMovies. "Jennifer Lawrence - Winter's Bone Interview." YouTube video, 7:18. June 8, 2010. www.youtube.com/watch?v=Hv7Sgrt_PXo.

_____. "X-Men: First Class Jennifer Lawrence Interview." YouTube video, 5:34. June 3, 2011. www.youtube.com/watch?v=F-Of53ou2Y8.

Valby, Karen. "'Hunger Games' director Gary Ross talks about 'the easiest casting decision of my life.'" *Entertainment Weekly*, March 17, 2011. www.ew.com/article/2011/03/17/hunger-games-gary-ross-jennifer-lawrence.

Wilkinson, Amy. "'Hunger Games' Casting Exclusive: Lionsgate Confirms Jennifer Lawrence As Katniss." *MTV*, March 17, 2011. www.mtv.com/news/2555422/hunger-games-jennifer-lawrence-lionsgate-confirms.

Zakarin, Jordan. "Jennifer Lawrence's Career Journey, From 'Bill Engvall' to 'Hunger Games.'" *The Hollywood Reporter*, March 22, 2012. www.hollywoodreporter.com/heat-vision/jennifer-lawrence-career-bill-engvall-winters-bone-hunger-games-303297.

INDEX

Page numbers in **boldface** are illustrations. Entries in **boldface** are glossary terms.

Academy Awards, **4**, 5, 11, 31, **31**, 54
    nominations, 28–29, 52, 55, 79–80
    wins, 6–7
Adams, Amy, 53, 55, 58, 66
aesthetic, 77
alchemist, 38
American Hustle, 52–53, 55, 57-58, 64, **66,** 84
antagonist, 36
aplomb, 22
awards, other, 23–24, 84

Bale, Christian, 53, 55, 66–67, **66**
Beaver, The, 34, **34**
Bill Engvall Show, The, **18**, 19–20
Burning Plain, The, 21, **23**, 24, 29, 44, 73

Cooper, Bradley, 49–50, **50**, 52–53, 55, 64, 66, **66**, 77

cyber attack, 58

directorial debut, 23
Dunham, Lena, 58, 67, **67**, 69

early life,
    brothers, 7, 9–10, 13–14, **17**
    family, 12–14, **17**, 32, 54, 68
    hometown, *see* Louisville,
    father, 7, 13–14, 16, **17**
    mother, 6–7, 12, 16, 25, 32
eponymously, 19
Everdeen, Katniss, 35, 40–42, **40**, 43, 48, **56**, **74**, 84

facetiousness, 9
fandom, 43
franchise, 16, 33, 35–36, 57, 59, 72–73, 83, 86

Golden Globe awards, **79–80**, 82, 84

nominations, 79
wins, 80

hackers, 58
House at the End of the Street, 44, 84
Hunger Games, The, 32, 35, 38–40, **40**, **43**, 50, 71–74, **74**, 84–86, **85**
Hunger Games: Catching Fire, The, 72
Hunger Games: Mockingjay Part 1, The, 72
Hunger Games: Mockingjay Part 2, The, 71–72, 75

impasse, 7
indie film, 33, 35, 47

Joy, 64, **70**, 71, 75–76, 80

Louisville, KY, 12, 16, 41, 68

Mangano, Joy, 75–77
MTV Movie Awards, 84
muse, 25
Mystique, 35–38, **37**, 83, 86

nadir, 72

one-up, 16
Oscars, *see* Academy Awards

pay equality, 63, 65, 69
persona, 57

perturbed, 45
pilot, 13
Poker House, The, 23–24
portmanteau, 54
purportedly, 65

Q&A, 54, 68

Renner, Jeremy, 65–67, **66**
Russell, David O., **47**, 47–53, 55, 64, 71, 76–78, **79**, 80

salaries, 58, 63, 65
satirical, 58
Schumer, Amy, **80**, 80–82
screwball comedy, 55
Silver Linings Playbook, **5**, 6, 16, **46**, 49, **50**, 51, 53, 84
soft reboot, 36

television, 14–17, 19, 21, 24, 84
Tomlin, Lily, 47–48, 77, 80
trifecta, 57

Winter's Bone, 25, **26**, 28–29, 31, 33, 42, 68, 84

X-Men: Apocalypse, 36, 83, 86
X-Men: Days of Future Past, 36, 83
X-Men: First Class, 36, 38, 75, 83

ABOUT THE AUTHOR

Madelyn Beauregarde was born in Beaver Dam, Wisconsin. She enjoys writing in her spare time and on subjects she cares about. Her older sister, Constance, is also a writer.